AN EXECUTIVE'S PRIMER ON

Public Relations

BY JOHN F. BUDD, JR.

Chilton Book Company

Philadelphia   New York   London

An Executive's Primer on Public Relations

Foreword

This book grows out of some twenty years of exposure to the diverse public relations problems of industry, and is seasoned by experiences gained in coping with this mixed lot. The opportunities, the headaches and the successes were all met with under the businesslike auspices of Carl Byoir & Associates. It is, however, my book and reflects my own thoughts, opinions and biases. This is as it must be. For, unlike such professions as law, whose statutory form minimizes absolute dependence on human decision, public relations is, above all else, personal judgment and experience. The methodology and techniques are only tools—to be used or misused. Essentially, this is why public relations as discussed in the clinical atmosphere of a university classroom, and so neatly codified in college texts, often seems incompatible with conditions encountered in real-life situations—even naïve. Whatever the merits or faults of this book, they're mine and not my employer's.

But, of course, this book would still not exist if the panjandrums of CB&A hadn't the confidence to expose the fledglings of their organization to the firing line, where experiences are gained and stored for another day. As public relations practice becomes more sophisticated, the need for greater depth and dimension in academic training grows proportionately. But it is still a truth that no classroom can fully prepare a candidate for the daily cataclysm of decisions he'll ultimately have to make.

You can't really learn what to do and what not to do in a strike situation, for example, until you've sat on the hard-backed chairs in a mediator's dreary office; until you've lived on hotel food for so long that you've memorized the menu; until you've flinched at the violence on a picket line; until you've cried, in the frustration of trying to get your side told in the newspapers, and until you realize that usually it doesn't matter, because strikes are never settled in public print and headlines. The chance and opportunity to learn by doing, by seeing, by analyzing and even by second-guessing oneself, is the priceless asset that a problem-solving organization like Byoir uniquely offers.

Public relations has, I admit, generated a lot of semantic nonsense. None of this, however, can be traced to the Byoir organization. It is a no-nonsense shirt-sleeved operation, cast in the mold of one of its creators, Gerry Swinehart. This witty Hoosier pragmatist could wield an inter-office memo like a stiletto, to impale some fuzzy thinker or to deflate a top-heavy ego. Advice had to stand the test of action, and beleaguered was the poor soul who passed judgment without the know-how to execute his words of wisdom. Yet, Gerry also had the tolerance to accept mistakes that were honestly created, and he patiently added lesson upon lesson to my own personal inventory of experiences. Complementing Gerry's blunt forthrightness has always been the perceptive analysis and logic spinning off with computer-like precision from CB&A's chairman, George Hammond. Always stimulating, always a thought ahead of you, this restless perfectionist has been the prime prod that's brought CB&A to the apex among professional counseling firms. His influence has guided my counseling and my experiences, and therefore, much of this book. If this book is as easily read as it is intended to be, a longtime friend, colleague and tutor, John Stahr, editorial director of the group, will be pleased. It is typical of John that although immersed in his own book creation, he took time to read every one of the 70,000 words in this book—sharpening, honing, challenging, and in every sense improving its clarity.

A word, too, about my colleagues, a creative band of individualists who consider a public relations text as stimulating as watching paint dry, and as informative as a three-year-old release. Nevertheless, they indulged me; let me pick their brains; provided me with gutty case history examples, and although they will deny it—encouraged me to write this book. "Tell it as it really is," they said, and this is precisely what I've tried to do.

And, finally, the traditional word for the wife. I suspect that no greater goad has a writer than to be unpublished while his wife works on her third book and doodles with a fourth. Little did Elaine realize, however, that in overcoming my inertia it would cost her the only quiet, secluded room in the house (her hideaway office), as my fragile creativity demanded concentration—and undisturbed comfort.

JOHN F. BUDD, JR.

Locust Valley, New York
August, 1968

Preface—Separating the Fact from the Fantasy

Businesses in the United States currently spend more than $5 billion a year on public relations. By any yardstick it's big business; some 100,000 people are engaged in it, and its principal trade association ranks high in the nation with a membership of some 6,000 practitioners in 63 cities, Puerto Rico and 28 countries. At least 3,200 new practitioners will be needed annually by the 1970's.

Of the 750 largest corporations in the U.S., at least 630, or 84 per cent, have some kind of formal public relations activity, and departments charged with this responsibility are said to be spawning at the rate of 100 a year. This is about twice the rate of growth of the nation's colleges.

A good portion of this new activity is ineffective—perhaps as much as 50 per cent, I estimate—wasted and watered down by myriad factors. Although its ancestry goes back to the tap roots of this nation—two of the authors of the Federalist Papers, Alexander Hamilton and James Monroe, are credited by historian Professor Broadus Mitchell with the best public relations job in history in selling the Constitution—public relations remains, as Bernard P. Gallagher said in a special report, "one of the most confused, diffused and refused tools of management." A catechism of its shortcomings would be too parochial; it is sufficient to center on the amateurish direction, unrealistic budgeting and poor planning or lack of any planning at all. But, often, too, this work pursues the wrong objectives, perhaps a product of the semantic curtain existing between public relations and top management. Often its responsibilities and authority are so pigeonholed, or diffused in the organizational maze that its impact can never be felt. But, as Gallagher points out, when used intelligently and creatively it touches every phase of a company's operations.

Why, then, is so much of this new tool of modern, enlightened management squandered? It's because much of the acceptance of public relations is more theoretical than factual—more lip service than staff service. Author L. L. L. Golden says it more simply: "Today's corporation has the kind of public relations that management wants; no better, nor worse." This does not mean that managers are executive drop-outs, flunking social science; there are logical reasons for this general lack of sophistication about public relations. To rise to the top of today's complex business machine demands the dedicated concentration of a specialist. There's neither time nor inclination to worry about the nuances of the public's attitudes. But, once at the top, it becomes a priority consideration; perhaps for the first time, the businessman has time to realize that his corporation has had to take on such new roles as educator, philanthropist and community citizen—while continuing to make a profit.

A businessman who can intuitively spot the weakness in a sales program, a financing campaign, an engineering project or even in an advertising campaign, finds it difficult—even frustrating—to be that perceptive about his company's public relations activity. So he delegates the responsibility, or at least the mechanical authority, for its execution. Yet, he is never completely satisfied that it's producing what it should.

Even if he should agree with the banker who maintains that the whole apparatus and function of public relations, like a computer, is no better than what goes into it in the first place, how does he judge what to feed it?

What should public relations offer? How, where and by whom?

Answers, of course, exist in the more than 1,000 books and booklets published on or about public relations, but they're too wordy for an executive interested simply in getting insight to help decide whether or not his company's public relations staff is adequate. He needs a guide to what to look for in his public relations director. But not one so full of jargon that it needs decoding. He wants to know in plain words, what should public relations' function and place in the organization be: what it can do—what it should do—for the company, in sales support, neighborhood relations, labor relations, financial relations. What would be a realistic budget? What is the proper public relations–advertising department relationship?

The book will give the answers to these questions in straightforward, no-nonsense style. There are no wordy side-excursions into the mechanics of, or cook-bookery of, public relations, or any pious preaching about public responsibility and social philosophy. The sole objective is to give the busy executive a realistic view of basic functions of public relations that can be absorbed in an evening's or a week end's reading. It is, in fact, a few hours' investment which can save interminable hours of office time to arrive at the same point of evaluation.

There's no mystique about it; skills and techniques of professionals are essential, yes, but it's not an occult science. As might be expected, public relations people are their own worst problem when it comes to communicating their functions. The corporate prose of the public relations man is too often gobbledygook and jargon.

A NEW PERSPECTIVE

Public relations is, above all else, a matter of perspective. Given the right viewpoint, the professional tools and techniques can be employed effectively. Without this perspective, too often they are squandered. In simple English, this book will give the businessman an insider's view of what to expect from his public relations activity—and what *his* responsibilities are to his public relations director. This latter may sound preachy but Lewis A. Lapham, vice chairman and director of Banker's Trust Company, confessed that he'd learned "in tears and sweat if not in blood, that public relations philosophy, inspiration and action must flow from the top. For no matter how skillful the public relations techniques and technicians, they simply cannot succeed if top management is unaware of or sidesteps its responsibilities in describing its place in the community and in defining its philosophy and its objectives."

No company, of course, is without public relations. Even when not a formal corporate practice, it is an informal by-product of normal relationships of people with people. The term itself is a grammatical sleight-of-hand—it's really *publics* relations, as diverse as the company's own dealings with different groups of people—employees, customers, neighbors, the government, stockholders, ad infinitum.

It is quite true that many executives have an intuitive sense for the right thing to do to keep this relationship harmonious. Strong-willed and confident, they hire former newsmen to handle the mechanics of communication, and this base is considered covered.

IS ANYBODY LISTENING?

Even for those imbued with the judgment or "feel" for a healthy rapport, the process of communicating this is more complex than simply "having good intentions." For one thing there is the inescapable matter of having the time. It's been estimated that the average American executive spends 80 per cent of his work week talking and only 20 per cent reading, writing and planning. This leaves only overtime for the heart of the executive function: thinking creatively, planning, delegation and review. But it also goes deeper. Certainly U.S. Steel had the right intentions and thought them compatible with the public's long term interest when it raised steel prices three-and-a-half per cent on April 11, 1962, only to arouse the fury of three government agencies and have national figures, led by President Kennedy, castigate the company publicly for "its contempt of 185 million Americans." Certainly General Motors built reliable cars and believed that the public agreed they were, until Ralph Nader devoted 42 pages of his book *Unsafe at Any Speed* to an attack on the safety of one of its biggest-selling cars, the Corvair. Certainly the pharmaceutical industry believed its drug prices were fair and equitable and a bargain for the public, until Senator Estes Kefauver launched his probe in 1959, and as recently as 1967, three drug companies were convicted of anti-trust.

Hundreds of other instances of misunderstandings are recorded only in the prolonged labor difficulty, in some friendly letters from stockholders, or in the most crushing retaliation of all, the withdrawing of support in the marketplace. Communication seems deceptively simple; but it's a tricky course to run without professional guidance. The competent public relations man—who can see and hear *both* ways—can be an effective middleman in achieving the maximum from this communication process. He's an expert in communication—but his expertise is not restricted to skill at a typewriter, or eloquence on his feet; he listens, he absorbs, he analyzes, he translates and he counsels.

Since this book is written for management, and not the practitioner, I reassure you again that it will lean heavily toward the "whys" of public relations and not the "how to's." The methodology is the concern of the public relations director; management's concern is that the tools-of-the-trade be used effectively.

Finally, I hope to give lexicographic last rites to such

smart aleck definitions of public relations as "higher hokum" or "Dale Carnegie writ large," because it is a legitimate and essential trade, necessitated by the complexity of modern life and the workings of an open society. "It is growing," says Professor Seymour Martin Lipset of Harvard, "because there is ever more direct communication between power and people."

You'll find no definition of public relations in this text. The book itself is the best description I can give. Reading it is the most effective way to learn about it. The only practical test of its impact will be the stimulation it gives you and the fresh perspective it may create.

Contents

Contents

An Executive's Primer on Public Relations

CHAPTER ONE

What Management Should Expect from Public Relations

The assignment page from the log of a department of one of the nation's major metals producers contains the following entries:

For four days and nights served as principal corporate source for reports on one of the company's bauxite ships fired on by Cuban aircraft.

Presented management options on probable impact of a price increase.

Outlined for the sales department a program and a budget for tabloid newspapers tailored for visiting customers.

Conducted a community survey of opinion on a plant the company was considering buying.

Recommended and carried out a program to counter a threat of annexation of plant property by an adjoining community.

Advising the tax department on procedure for getting public support to oppose new business taxes.

Translating from technical idiom into general language details of a new data processing center.

Recommending an air quality control program to top management.

Tracing the source of a persistent rumor (that the

1

company was going to buy and rebuild a ghost town in the Southwest), and squashing it.

Counteracting rumors, just prior to Passover, that a company product was made with animal oils.

Discovering and reporting in detail the operation of the Russian and Red Chinese aluminum industries.

The source of the potpourri of services? Sales? Engineering? Executive staff? Nope, they're all from public relations inventory. What's more, Donald B. McCammond, general director of public relations for Reynolds Metals Company, describes the diverse activities as "bread-and-butter, day-to-day line operations of the public relations staff." Those who equate public relations with publicity will feel uneasy at the lack of any press release activity in this smorgasbord of work.

But this is understandable, because few jobs in American business management are as loosely defined as that of the public relations director. Largely because management itself doesn't really know what it wants or should expect from the public relations man, he is often left to fend for himself, to establish his own criteria for performance. He also develops his own responsibilities and attempts to create acceptance for self-defined authority. Meanwhile he has to wedge his way, somehow, into the corporate hierarchy, which generally fights the intrusion with all the stubborn dedication of white corpuscles attacking germs.

Even sophisticated managements with an advanced sensitivity to the need to improve the company's relationships with its customers, neighbors, legislators, employees, stockholders and so on, are vague, even naïve, as to how this should be accomplished—or for that matter, how much it should cost.

And if they should successfully resist the temptation to choose the company extrovert as their public relations head (John, in sales, because "he knows the company, gets along well with people and is energetic"), they are completely at sea in evaluating either performance or public relations people. Compounding the difficulty is the superficial savoir faire of almost all public relations people. Be they of good, bad or indifferent capabilities they are all articulate and masters of self-confidence. They know just how much communication jargon to sprinkle into their conversations or reports to give a flavor of expertise, and they exude just the right touch of charm and self-assurance. Being a candidate and not an incumbent affords even greater license for fearless and audacious talk about the wonders public relations will work—often heady conversation for the conservative executive who wishes that his company (and maybe he, himself) could receive more recognition!

Executives who seek professional improvement, or action, in any phase of their business need to know, one, what they want to accomplish and, two, some yardsticks by which to appraise the competence of the men to whom they entrust this assignment.

It is a corollary of our times that businessmen, precise and nerveless as computers in making major decisions daily in sales, manufacturing, engineering, financing or marketing, will abandon their proven formulas when it comes to public relations. "You have to accept the fact," George Hammond, chairman of Carl Byoir & Associates, told business executives at a communications forum sponsored by the economic advisers, Mackay-Shields, "that public relations investment can in many different ways improve the P&L statement and increase net worth over a span of years, just as other investment programs do. If you want to build facilities to accomplish this, the questions of adequacy, alternative approaches, management and specialized skills have to be answered just as realistically as any of the more conventional investments."

A partner of one energetic management counseling firm, Gardner W. Heidrick, of highly regarded Heidrick & Struggles, says that while there's been a notable increase in searches for public relations executive within the last couple of years, job descriptions are still more nebulous than for

3

their counterparts in top management. He believes this is so primarily because the function is not well understood, because it does not always have the stature it should and because the responsibilities vary all over the lot.

INTUITION VS EXPERTISE

Despite the mushrooming growth of corporate public relations consciousness and the general acceptance of the impact public opinion has on the success or failure of an enterprise, management still too often relies on instincts and intuitions alone in setting up an internal organization to deal with its publics. This does not mean that their judgment will mislead them; indeed, in many instances they correctly interpret a problem in this area and will instinctively sense the proper course of action to take. This is one of the deceptive aspects of public relations. Much of it is just good common sense operating from a firm base of familiarity with factors peculiar to a company.

But the technology of communication, the new mobility of our people, the so-called "knowledge revolution"—all of these have combined to accelerate the speed of transmitting ideas and information. The competition for the attention of the public is intense. No company has any exclusive hold on the attention of any group; even its shareholders divide their loyalty among many interests.

The net effect of this is that the dimensions of the situation have grown beyond the ability of non-professionals to cope with it. Executives, however strong their visceral sensations, need expert advice on how to deal with their publics.

What are the characteristics of the expert public relations man? The complete public relations man is an uncommon man. He will be aggressive, yet humble; he will be curious, restless and perennially dissatisfied, yet know the value of

4

patience; he will be a non-conformist but will fit in smoothly as part of the company team; he will be something of an idealist with a realist's check-rein in hand; he will be unyieldingly demanding of his own performance but reasonably tolerant of error in others; and he will be enthusiastic.

A fictional profile? A paragon of corporate virtue? Not really. Such people exist in healthy quantities. The trick is to know what to look for and to recognize it when you find it. This problem is much harder when too narrow a perspective is applied to the job.

So we begin with a point of view, a philosophy.

THE QUID PRO QUO OF PUBLIC RELATIONS

It's this simple: You hire or appoint a public relations executive because you want something to happen—you want corporate inertia to be overcome, perhaps. You may not be capable of being any more specific than that. But you sense need for improvement in this broad, rather amorphous region of better relationships with all of the internal and external groups affecting your company. At the same time, you are not looking to buy a revolution, or to stimulate one. Nevertheless, some healthy evolutionary changes are in order.

Even if your present interest in and awareness of the need for improvement in public relations direction is triggered by some immediate problem—a disastrous strike, an awkward community problem or even irritation over all the publicity a competitor is receiving—you sense there are other sides to the problem. You would like some expert guidance, to be told what to do, not asked.

Raymond H. Mulford exposed the sensitive and vulnerable aspects of corporate management when he pointed out that "business is understandable but not understood," and therein lies the danger of restrictions, regulations and interference that could damage any enterprise. Certainly after our experiences of the past few years, after the riots in Watts, Detroit and Newark and the turbulence still existing in dozens of other cities, how corporate social responsibility ties into the healthy pursuit of profits should be broadly understood and recognized.

Thus, in the context of today's social and business environment, what the head of a business should reasonably expect from his public relations officer goes dimensions beyond the bread-and-butter skills of newswriting and publicity.

Fundamentally, you need bright, fluid men, people aware that the establishment isn't sacrosanct, that it is as fallible as human beings. And you need people who have nerve enough to express their convictions and intelligence enough to have alternatives, not just criticisms.

One of the most successful public relations organizations in the nation is that of the American Telephone and Telegraph Company, and it's the largest. There are some 640 employees in the department, for an enterprise that has 850,000 employees and 50 million customers. Its vice chairman, John D. DeButts, says flatly that management should expect continuous criticism from the public relations man of the status quo of the business. This criticism, he says, should be based on sensitivity to the environment, on accurate knowledge of what is going on. Author Golden sees it as ". . . an industrial DEW line which will alert management to new trends in public thinking, to new desires, to new demands which can affect the successful conduct of business."

The point should be made here, I think, that all of this enlightened view is not new-found religion brought on by strikes, civil rights violence, urban disorders or widespread criticism of industrial pollution of air, water and land. For example, eight years ago Monroe Wells, vice president of operations for Reynolds Metals Company, told a Virginia public relations conference that his company had some very specific views on what it expected of its public relations personnel. Fundamentally, he said, it expects public relations

6

to keep the company informed. Informed of what? Of a number of things, and he ticked them off. "Of what is being said about the company in any part of the world. Of what is being said or written about our industry. Of what the competition is doing. Of what developments are taking place that might threaten our business, our operations, locally, nationally, and internationally. Of any number of things going on, or that may occur to affect our continued success.

"And that is only half of what we expect. We expect our public relations people to assist . . . in presenting our side of any given controversy . . . in preparing material to keep the public informed . . . and to provide the best advice on means of forestalling criticism, or the situations that breed criticism." An all-encompassing inventory, by any measure.

The relationship between the public relations officer and the top management of a company differs from those of other department heads and other specialists. For one thing, the chief executive officer is also the chief executive officer of the public relations function— at least in principle. He sets the tone and creates the policy and the environment that determines whether or not it is used creatively or intelligently. So, between public relations man and chief executive there needs to exist the highest level of personal and professional understanding and mutual appreciation. This is not so critical in other executive relationships. This empathy, or mutual respect, is a chemical reaction; rarely can it be created artificially. As with any formula, the ingredients must be measured carefully. For example:

Management has the right to expect, at the outset, that its public relations adviser have the qualities of a manager. This means he must be able to define problems and opportunities, set goals, plan ahead, measure results, control costs, and manage people.

He must be able to think pragmatically about the job at hand and abstractly about the long-range objectives of his function.

7

He must thoroughly learn management's objectives and recognize that while he may influence policy, he does not *set* policy and that his objectives are irrelevant until management agrees with him.

He must know what's going on in the world around him, and have enthusiasm for learning and the ability to relate all of this to the company's objectives.

Management will expect him to submit recommendations for action that will put the company squarely in the position of doing what it should do under whatever circumstances set the parameters.

Banker Lapham says that, since information is said to be the soul of enterprise, he expects his public relations people to comprise the department of "clear communication." It's their job, he says, to see that the corporation communicates simply, directly and factually.

It therefore becomes obvious that the basal metabolism of public relations is high and it is keyed to action. It is the means of improving public understanding, of adjusting to it, if necessary, of informing it, or of winning it over. None of these goals can be accomplished without overt action in some form.

How do you recognize whether or not your public relations man has these qualifications? Or, if you're seeking a new one, how do you judge the credibility of the oral résumé delivered with such confidence?

The state-of-the-art being an inexact one, the measure of a public relations man cannot satisfactorily be taken by conventional means. But there are some telltale things to look for, and some perceptive questions to ask that will give a fairly accurate accounting of his capabilities and potential.

ANATOMY OF A PUBLIC RELATIONS MAN

A key consideration in weighing the qualifications of a public relations director is whether his background (or in the case of an incumbent, his performance) confirms an ability to be an activist. One should be wary of the theoreticians. They can be captivatingly reassuring, but the gap between theory and practice is generally a chasm. Textbook public relations theory sets a high tone and suggests methods and measures that would be effective only under the most ideal circumstances. These do not exist and never will.

So there is a practicality gap. Does your candidate recognize this? Or does he smoothly discourse upon systems and procedures, betraying an isolation from the realities of corporate life?

Drawing upon 37 years of counseling experience, George Hammond emphasizes that public relations is an "apprenticeship business." Academic study can sharpen a man's insight of social behavior and sociological disciplines, but only experience gives it the practical test. Public relations skill in dealing with people in general, with employees, the community, writers, reporters and other news media people is gained only through participation. It cannot be acquired through case study work or through problem-solving charades. It is learned by doing.

Look for this experience, go behind the superficialities of the résumé and determine precisely what degrees of involvement the candidate has had in typical public relations situations.

Has he worked with a staff, or has he been a one-man show? Has he handled a budget of any consequence? What about his earlier programs? Is there any depth to his planning? Are his proposals specific or couched in generalities? Does his record show that he generally reacts to situations or does he create situations and opportunities in which to act? In short, is the initiative his, or is he simply a slave to developments in whose origin he has played no part?

Has he, in planning previous assignments, defined his objectives; researched or analyzed them; charted a plan of activity and timing; blueprinted an organization appropriate to the size of the job; executed his program; reappraised

9

results, etc.? One should not be misled by the creative overtones of public relations activity or glib comments that you can't program human behavior or individual attitudes.

True, public relations is decidedly more creative than, say, accounting. It must be flexible and operate with a high degree of opportunism. Granted, further, that nobody can fully predict a year's events—occasions that draw heavily upon public relations' inputs and reaction-quotient.

This does not mean that it bears a charmed life, free from the discipline of organized planning. Far from it. For it is only through the rigors of such discipline that a maximum effort can ever be realized. Without specific targets and timetable, public relations staffs quickly drown in a sea of noncreative minutiae, or wallow about the company doing unimportant jobs for lazy product managers.

Can your man write? Not long-winded essays, but friendly letters and effective interoffice memos? Is he skilled in the straightforward, succinct use of plain words that quickly convey a message? Your associates may tell you that you don't need a publicity man, and perhaps you don't. But unless your candidate has the capability of fast, tight, skillful writing, the program will wobble like a two-legged stool. The written word is the "bread and butter" tool of any working public relations program. And taking college courses in English does not qualify a man as a writer. Look for some form of professional writing skill.

How effective do you think he'd be if he had to delegate to a subordinate the drafting of the president's letter in the annual report, or your speech before the Rotary, or the development of a position paper during a tense labor negotiation? It would be foolish to compromise on this requirement. Read some samples of his writing. Convince yourself.

No point in asking him about his relationship with news media; he'll gloss over that with anecdotes about the press conferences he's handled, the press tours he's organized, the corporate birthday programs he's devised. He'll know all the radio people, the magazine people, the chief editorial writers, etc. Whether it's true or not isn't critical *if* he's the right man, for if he is, he'll make any contacts valuable to the company's interests in short order, even if he doesn't know where the local paper is published. And if that's the case, he'll be candid enough to say so if he's the right man.

Get over to an area in which you have some knowledge yourself. Ask him what he thinks the proper relationship should be with employees, shareholders and customers, with vendors, community officials and the financial community. Weigh his answers carefully. If they make sense to you they're probably sound.

Ask him what experience he's had working on stock-holder reports, employee publications, speeches, booklets. How has he coordinated his programs with other internal departments of the company? To whom did he report? A good clue here. If he reported to sales or advertising or to nobody higher than a vice president, you've a reliable sign that his impact was less than major on the company's public relations conduct.

The choice of the right person for any job is part science and part hunch or educated guess. Public relations adds no new dimension to this perennial problem, just a degree of unfamiliarity.

Perhaps with these words and those that follow, the public relations man will be so well defined that you'll be able to spot a good one as readily as you can recognize a born salesman.

Bear in mind that what you are asking for on the bottom line of public relations is sound, realistic recommendations that will put your company squarely in the position of doing what it ought to do.

This means that what you are actually expecting, deButts' says, is "that public relations will demand the most of management." Has your public relations director, or candidate for that job, the guts and the expertise to do this?

11

An Executive's Primer on Public Relations

There are no better criteria to evaluate your public relations quotient than the responsibilities one of the nation's oldest and largest public relations counseling firms, Carl Byoir & Associates, sets down as its own yardsticks. In its view, a diversified public relations program must be geared to satisfactorily execute the following requirements:

Develop confidence of stockholders, analysts, employees, customers, and suppliers in the management group.

Present a convincing case in a major controversy.

Obtain public understanding and vocal support for the company's position in a critical labor situation.

Project the broader concept of a company that has diversified.

Conduct a swift and efficient drive for stockholder, trade and consumer appreciation of a major merger, expansion or acquisition.

Ensure quick recognition of a company's new corporate name and understanding of its significance.

Transmit effectively to legislators and the public an organization's views on pending legislation.

Generate understanding and support for policy changes.

Obtain cooperation of employees and the community upon moving to a new location.

Make products, policies, or management better known.

Introduce a new product.

Explain the position of management in a proxy solicitation or controversy.

Overcome adverse publicity arising out of litigation.

Capitalize fully on a success achieved by the organization.

CHAPTER TWO

The Role of the
Public Relations Director

Let's get down to cases. What, specifically, should the public relations director do? Whether you're hiring one or concerned that the job as now being executed falls short, the same touchstones apply.

We've established that he's not a magician who will whitewash a spotted image. Nor is he a good-natured buffer who'll keep inquisitive reporters at arm's length. And, finally, we've seen that there's more to his job than simply generating a flow of positive-sounding stories about the company so that attention will be diverted from its shortcomings.

The really qualified public relations director has a great deal more depth than these superficial definitions imply. He performs a pivotal managerial function in the company, yet he generally has no policy-making powers, only the power of persuasion.

He is fundamentally a catalyst. Upon his initiative management takes action to obtain as favorable a consensus from its various publics as is reasonable to expect. This latter limitation is hard for some public relations people to accept. But the fact remains that what is best for the shareholder may not be best for society and, conversely, there are situations where what is best for society may be incompatible with the interests of the company and its shareholders. The skill at resolving

13

such a conflict is really what public relations is all about. The idealist who equates social good with the basic objectives of the company without regard for the latter's need to show a profit is ill-suited for the job.

This is not a matter of ultimatums. Nor does the public relations practitioner withdraw in frustration. Being a pragmatist he accepts the fact that, however skilled he is, his best efforts will probably generate no better than an acceptable balance—a broad acceptance, arrived at by the majority, that the company is doing its level best and that it is acting honestly, reasonably and with awareness of its responsibilities to society.

TEN-POINT VALUE INDEX OF A PUBLIC RELATIONS DIRECTOR

Public relations, by its broadest definition, so permeates the corporate structure that some public relations officers feel that only the most sweeping, generalized programming can fulfill its vast responsibilities. Or, at any rate, they feel that this is a beautiful rationale for the kind of vague programming and activity that, like Chinese food, seems to fill the bill but later makes you question whether or not it really did.

If you're wondering if your public relations man is really worth his salt, see how he scores on the following test.

PR Value Index

1. Does your public relations director's typical year's program deal with specifics instead of vague and generally altruistic outlines of the year ahead?   Yes_____   No_____

> (If it does, good. If it doesn't, watch out. He may lack the creativity, or the initiative to plan ahead

14

or has never dealt with the realities of such specific programming.)

2. Is his budget request always the same size?
Yes_____ No_____

(Would be appropriate only if your company hasn't grown, either.)

3. Does your company's public relations director come to you (top management) with ideas and suggestions, or do you have to request them? Yes_____ No_____

(If he has to be summoned he lacks either the ideas or the courage to suggest them; in either case he's shortchanging the company.)

4. How often has the public relations director disagreed —out loud—with top management? Can he say no? Has he?
Often_____ Sometimes_____ Never_____

(Since no company has perfect public relations, it is inconceivable that a skilled man in this sensitive post will never find an action to question, a decision to challenge. It's not a question of his being a gadfly but, rather, one of his being an objective counterbalance.)

5. Does the public relations director ever ask embarrassing questions—or provocative questions?
Sometimes_____ Never_____

(The most expensive commodity in a modern company is a bland, "never rock the boat" public relations mentality.)

6. Is your public relations director really involved in the company's daily actions or does he delegate all but liaison with top management? Yes_____ No_____

15

(Pragmatic skills make more substantial contributions to the company's public relations posture than theoretical ones.)

7. Does your public relations director write and speak with fresh ideas, without clichés and safe homilies?

Yes____ No____

(How he expresses ideas is a measure of the quality of the original thinking he's capable of putting into programs for the company.)

8. How many programs or activities has your director suggested that relate to events in the news?

Some____ None____

(If his programs never touch such current topics as urban poverty, education, consumerism, etc., regardless of whether or not such have been asked for, you can be sure your rapport with your publics could be improved.)

9. Can you always find your man in his office?

Yes____ No____

(Like dieting, the only way to succeed in public relations is to push yourself away from the table [in this case the desk] and get out where the action is, regularly.)

10. Does his department reflect the status quo, or has it shown growth and change? Yes____ No____

(There's nothing static about public relations, either from a technical point of view or from the creative aspects; stability here is likely to signify sterility.)

Unless you can answer in the affirmative in at least five instances (questions 2 and 9 should both be "no"), your company's public relations needs some overhauling. These points do not so much reflect the deeds of public relations as they give an insight into your adviser's philosophy about relations.

They will show the basic attitude needed and give a sense of the pace that today's economic/social environment demands of the public relations man. Specific responsibilities vary, of course, from company to company. To say dogmatically that a public relations officer is lacking in something because he's not involved in stockholder relations or labor negotiations, for instance, would be misleading and unjust. In many companies these functions are capably handled by outstanding specialists. However, this does not mean that the public relations man has no responsibility for being aware of actions in these areas, because his own programs must be compatible with policies set in these areas. But he is not on front-line duty there.

Whatever the scope of the public relations assignment (and this should never remain static, but should be a growing, dynamic operation), it must live within the discipline of the following elements:

Research and analysis

Programming (detailed and specific)

Execution

Feedback or evaluation

It's pertinent to reiterate that the public relations director's responsibility encompasses more substance than merely expressing concern and awareness of the problems existing. Analysis is of little comfort or contribution unless it is accompanied by remedial plans, actions calculated to improve the situation.

Whether or not the public relations man has sound judgment and the basic common sense and wisdom to correctly identify the needs and the proper actions is, of course, a matter of hope. But so, too, is the new sales manager's program, the researcher's goal, etc. If the program rings true and sounds right, no doubt it is, but . . .

17

There still must be a system established for evaluating and measuring the effectiveness of the program, and this, too, is the public relations officer's responsibility. A prime one, too.

WHAT'S NEEDED IS SOME FEEDFORWARD

Public relations objectives, unlike the specific goals of sales, manufacturing and other internal departments, are not subject to the same insatiable need for change. Largely this is because objectives that are essentially sound in the first place rarely can be accomplished within twelve months. In terms of changing or markedly influencing opinions a year— even two or three—is but a micron of time.

Nevertheless, this does not give license to make each year's program a carbon copy of the one past. At the very least there has to be what in scientific vernacular is called feedforward. The noted British-born author and semanticist, I. A. Richards, coined this word as a reciprocal condition of what cybernetics and automation people call feedback. What feedforward means in the context of public relations programming is that the experiences, results, reactions and activities of one year's program must be fed forward to influence the planning of the next year's.

Elsewhere in this book we discuss in some detail just how much of the public relations activity can be measured. While it does not lend itself to quantitative measurement any more than its sister creative tool, advertising, it can be responsive to empirical study and analysis. For one thing you can identify the activities generated and what percentage of those originally programmed were completed; you can weigh how many new inputs were involved (which is one yardstick of the flexibilty, or lack of, in the programming); you can study the application and use of the budget and you can chart some of the results, such as printed reactions of outsiders (articles, stories in papers, reports or profiles on the company, etc.) and the tone and content of stockholder letters, customer responses, etc.

Much negative reaction to public relations was engendered by pioneer public relations expert Edward Bernays' description of the theory and practice of public relations as the "engineering of consent." Taken out of context this characterized public relations as a form of manipulation of people's minds. Nothing was further from Bernays' intent. He viewed public relations as a profession, and he submitted that its activities should be planned and executed in line with scientific principles, using the dispassionate approach and methods similar to those of the engineering profession.

In short, his way was to define the objectives, to bring all available resources to bear upon the problem, and to initiate action designed to improve the situation and then to review the results critically.

WHAT MAKES PUBLIC RELATIONS DIRECTORS TICK?

The public relations director should have integrity without becoming argumentative; he should have frankness, yet be tactful; he should be able to maintain his perspective despite his economic tie to the company, and to feel keenly his responsibilities even though, for a while, only he may identify them accurately.

Many men have all of these sterling qualities, yet fail, somehow, in applying their knowledge to the company's problems. Often they leave, of their own volition or by "suggestion," bewildered or embittered. Or they stay on and become "toothless tigers."

There's no pat answer why. The reasons may be as different as the fingerprints of the company executives involved. There are, however, lessons to be learned from the

19

more prevalent reasons cited for failure. A review of these may give some additional insight into what makes a public relations director tick.

Some public relations directors are, simply, too impatient. They're imbued with high ideals and such strong identification with social good that they cannot abide any action that isn't above reproach, regardless of profit-or-loss consequences. Life—business life, especially—isn't that simple. Much of what happens is a compromise, and the wise public relations man recognizes this and realistically strives to seek the optimum set of adjustments.

Many are too eager to escape what they regard as the tyranny of the typewriter. As the carpet goes on the floor and the art on the wall, the typewriter, dictionary, thesaurus, atlas, encyclopedia and book of quotations go out. Wrong! A profit-making company rarely can afford to have a theoretician operating on the firing line of public relations. The typewriter doesn't mean just publicity stories. It means annual reports; it means position papers on civic problems like water pollution; it means a memorandum to employees on strike, etc. *Show me a public relations man proud of his emancipation from the typewriter and I'll show you a man who's taken his first step to isolate himself from the realities of the job.*

And, finally, there's the executive drop-out, the public relations director who's run out of vinegar—and curiosity—but stays on, impeding the progress of both program and (younger) people. He's lost that fragile quality of enlightened dissatisfaction, that sixth sense of anticipation which "sees" the impact of such current actions as the civil rights movement, or the consumer's intensifying concern with service and quality. He feels that he's been a prophet without honor for so long that he no longer persists, no longer bothers to marshal his facts or to cogently present his arguments to management.

In the final analysis, the selection of a public relations

officer is much akin to choosing a wife. There are certain hereditary things you may look for; certain external signs you weigh in. Education and environmental influences concern you, too, but when it's all said and done either you feel or do not feel an empathy with the person in question, and that's the decisive thing!

PUBLIC RELATIONS: AN EXECUTIVE FUNCTION

The so-called "headhunting" phase, whether it's conducted within the corporation or without, does not create "instant public relations," because it can misfire immediately if the public relations adviser isn't strategically positioned in the inner hierarchy and supported by an adequate staff.

Public relations people are sometimes accused of egomania, but it is a fact that public relations is a function of top management. The public relations man is helpless unless the chief executive officer and the board of directors recognize the importance of the function and accord it appropriate weight in broad management deliberations. The public relations head should be an executive.

Vice presidents head the public relations operations of 630 of the largest U.S. companies. A year-end survey by *Public Relations News* indicated a growing trend among companies to list public relations executives among top management in their annual reports. Even when he's a notch below, as director of public relations, he still reports to the president. At Reynolds Metal the public relations staff is designated as an arm of the president's office; at AT&T the public relations director reports directly to the president, has immediate access to the chief executive, and uses it frequently during the day. At Standard Oil of New Jersey the publicity manager reports regularly to an executive vice president; periodically he is in contact with the president, and often

21

goes before the executive committee or the full board on public relations problems or to report on what the public relations department is doing.

Gardner Heidrick says corporations are recognizing more and more the importance of a sound public relations program, and therefore want a real professional rather than someone who has been developed from within.

Having the ear of management is an essential key, and a good public relations man doesn't overestimate his influence. He realizes that he doesn't set policy; but he can directly influence it by interpreting public attitudes toward policy and by offering judgments on the effects of policies on various publics before—not after—such policies are determined.

Participation in the decision-making process is the only way to get full value from the investment in public relations.

Effective public relations has a generous dosage of the "Chinese doctor" philosophy in it: emphasis is on the *prevention* rather than the *cure*. The company that involves its public relations man *after the fact* on management decisions will almost always be on the defensive in public relations. Communication will be one way—outwards. It can be done this way, of course (and in too many cases this is the practice, not the exception), but it's akin to talking without seeing or hearing. A corporation can no more afford to lose these two vital senses than can an individual.

The increased importance of sound public relations counsel has, obviously, resulted in a sharp rise in compensation for such men. It is not unusual for an experienced public relations officer of a large corporation to earn between $25,000 and $50,000, and there are instances where they've doubled this, earning in the $100,000 range. One survey made a couple of years ago showed 35 per cent of the public relations directors in companies with sales from $100 to $499 million, averaged, in income, between $20,000 and $30,000.

This same survey showed that the major shortcoming preventing the public relations department from operating at peak efficiency was inadequate personnel—ranking this over the traditional complaint of lack of management understanding.

It is a corporate paradox that sophisticated chief executive officers who demonstrate keen awareness of the need for keeping their companies "in tune" with prevailing attitudes, literally sabotage their own efforts by relegating public relations to small staffs with church-mice budgets. This generally limits the public relations operation to grinding out publicity, foreclosing on any broader contributions.

Several years ago, management of the Goodyear Tire & Rubber Co. suspected that its public relations department development had seriously lagged behind the overall growth of the company. A thorough analysis of the public relations program of the top 50 corporations showed that the most successful on the list also invested the most in their public relations programs. This, Goodyear decided, was more than coincidence. After a long search, it recruited an executive of one of the major public relations counseling firms, Robert H. Lane, a Penn State graduate and one-time editor for the Associated Press. Lane, 39, completely revamped the structure of the rubber company's public relations department over a two-year span. (Although, today, he's the first to acknowledge that the rebuilding program is still going on, this attests not to his sense of perfection as much as it does to the ever-changing nature of public relations itself.)

Here, again, statistics serve as a measure of the dynamics of growth, although they remain but a superficial indication of the depth and perceptiveness inherent in the planning.

Goodyear's concept of, and its evolution of, the public relations function parallels, to a large degree, the coming of age of the art as a top management function. In 1959, Lane inherited a staff of 10 people in Akron, two outside public relations agencies and a total budget of $400,000. Goodyear sales that year, it might be pertinent to note, were $1.3 billion. In 1968, Lane headed an international organization of 99 fulltime staff people (not including secretaries), located in 5 cities, plus six external public relations agencies abroad (covering Great Britain, Sweden, Japan, Malaysia, Turkey, Mexico, Switzerland, India and Italy). In addition, at 29 plant town communities the editors of the divisions' employee publications have been specially trained to serve as *ex-officio* members of the public relations department. The department itself published 60 employee newspapers; 29 dealer magazines; not one, but 5 annual reports; 5 field sales publications; 5 international newspapers, and 4 general magazines in 17 languages. Goodyear sales in 1968 were some $2.6 billion.

Lane, recently elected vice president (the first such public relations officer in the company's 70-year history, and the first in the industry to hold this title), operates this diversified ménage on a budget "in excess of $2 million," not including the operation of the fleet of Goodyear blimps.

Nine years ago, when the department was reorganized fully, as much as 75 per cent of its assignments were self-generated, the Goodyear official reports. Today, as a result of constantly expanding performance and ceaseless internal education on the role of public relations, the percentage has fallen off somewhat (probably around 50 per cent), as the Goodyear organization as a whole makes increasing demands on and use of the public relations department.

Budgets come in for detailed scrutiny in another chapter. The point should be made here, however, that budgets are generally substantial. A study of some 334 companies by Bernard Gallagher's organization a couple of years ago revealed the average annual budget to be $334,467. Companies that were industrially oriented tended to invest more ($462,000) than those in the service business ($268,000) while consumer oriented concerns spent an average of $281,000.

Perhaps the best practical yardstick of what comprises the total profile of a public relations adviser today is reflected in what the executive recruiters themselves seek in such a person. The following, from a leading management consulting firm, provides insight into what is expected, and what is offered in terms of compensation and basic job support.

Vice President—Public Relations

Company: One of the nation's leading trade associations, its membership is made up of approximately 150 leading United States manufacturers.

Location: New York.

Position: Reporting to the president, he will supervise a staff of nine, including several specialists in public and professional relations. In addition to controlling a budget of several hundred thousand dollars, he coordinates a national advertising campaign with an annual budget of $1,000,000. He will be personally concerned with stimulating and perpetuating good relations with all media.

Qualifications: The individual selected for this key position must be a proven public relations executive of the highest stature. He must be creative as well as an effective administrator. He will have a proven record of performance in all major aspects of public relations. Prior experience with a trade association representing a major industry, and some exposure to government relations, would be helpful.

Compensation and Future Prospects: Initial compensation will be in the $25,000 range, plus excellent fringe benefits. Future prospects are good.

CHAPTER THREE

Planning and Programming
(*How to Translate Theory into Practice*)

Public relations is a hard-nosed operation! No creative activity is more demanding. Substantial amounts of money are involved; corporate reputations are generally at stake; the ability of the company to operate without outside interference may be materially affected.

Although the objectives are usually specific, paradoxically the means for achieving them are vague and general. Further, the modus operandi is individual and customized for each company. So, too, one might say is advertising, sales or engineering. True, of course, but there is a recognized formula for procedure in these areas that applies in some measure to the appropriateness of current activity.

In public relations, not only are the parameters indistinct, but the radiations of almost any action have public relations impact. Obviously, what is needed is a sense of down-to-earth priorities.

This is the biggest hang-up for too many public relations people: the necessity to get down to cases and determine what is the best use of time and money; not what is the easiest or most pleasant, but how to get from A to B most efficiently. There's no room for fuzzy thinking or gentlemanly schedules. Public relations programming is an uncompromising disciplinarian! And because it serves as a service arm of any company it must not only have a specific activity schedule

26

to govern its pace but it must also be ready at any time, hour or place for those inevitable emergency situations a company is liable to face—a strike, a plant accident, stockholder suit, and so on.

What really distinguishes the public relations professional today from the more flamboyant, cutely ingenious publicity people is planning—careful planning based on research and analysis and pragmatic judgments. In this context, the article in the newspaper, however complimentary, is irrelevant unless it interlocks with other phases of the program.

Ken Ellington, who built one career as a top-notch radio newsman and later another as a public relations executive, says that "as is the case with an engineer's computer and a mechanic's wrench, public relations tools must serve a distinct purpose or there is not much sense in having them." Ellington, one-time vice president for Republic Aviation and now western regional executive for the Aircraft Industries Association, emphasizes that publicity is a much-misunderstood tool. "The mere counting up of column inches of news space serves very little purpose. What is important is what is said in a story and how that story plays its part in the over-all goals." That's the "bottom-line" of public relations action.

WHO SETS OBJECTIVES

A public relations program that just oozes into being, that grows without any clear-cut definition of its objectives to give it specific impetus, that exists without an examination of its course by the company's policy makers, will be a poor investment. Its architect, the public relations director, will probably become schizoid in frustrated efforts to please and to earn his keep.

Setting objectives is not as easy and routine as it appears. Applied psychological principles flatly state that people behave to satisfy their real motives, not the motives they should

27

A TYPICAL COMPANY, INC. PUBLIC RELATIONS—OPERATIONS FLOW

Role in Formulation of Policies on:

- Better mousetraps & associated product line
- Consumer applications
- Industrial applications
- Trends—R & D— retraps/containers
- Community/civic relationships
- Diversification
- Sales philosophy
  —Fair trade
  —Private vs national brand name

Crystallized Ideas → Specific Projects

RESEARCH

Whom do we want to influence?
What do they think now?
What do we want them to think?
How are we going to get them to do this?
- Specific targets
- Methods
- Raw materials
- Related materials
- Who is to do what, where and when?

PRODUCTION

1 Specific messages
2 Revisions
3 Company review
4 Revisions
5 Company approval

DISTRIBUTION

- Coverage
- Time Factors
- Coordination
- Comprehensive
- External
- Internal
- Geographical
- Continuity
- Economy
- Salesmanship
- Specialized
- Experience and Contacts

Stockholders

- Employees
- Customers
- Suppliers
- Distributor dealers
- Board of health
- Plant communities
- Competitors
- Government
- Education
- Scientific associations

RESEARCH

Carl Byoir & Associates, Inc.

Typical planning guide for public relations activity would follow this operations flow. Commencing left to right: Policy is established first, forming the basis for ideas and activities which are honed, evaluated and re-evaluated on the basis of applied research, finally blueprinted as to production, release and distribution to those publics the company concerns itself with. The concept of "feedforward" comes into play regularly as reactions and measures of results are digested and fed back into the creative process to "keep it in tune."

have. People are perverse: they have their own ideas of what they want and stubbornly refuse to be moved by appeals to motives which other people think they have or should have. Many companies and their public relations directors make serious mistakes by ignoring this principle. Far too many organizations act before determining the motives to which they can successfully appeal.

As public relations becomes more professional there is a corresponding increase in scientific research into what people think, their attitudes and their interests. Fifty-one per cent of the 250 companies studied in a special analysis by Robert W. Miller of The American University said that they regularly conducted public opinion or attitude polls, and the majority of the executives—46 per cent—said they were personally involved in the survey evaluation.

There are many practical examples. At the top, there's AT&T. The sheer size of the customer body, 50 million customers, dictates some formal method of surveying their attitudes. One means is the annual Customer Attitude Trend Study; the most recent one returned 80,000 completed questionnaires. A five-year "key publics" research project, opening with detailed attitude research on college students, covering 57 campuses, provided unparalleled insight into student views. This pioneering effort will explore independently each of the key publics which make up the total customer body.

Republic Aviation, on the other hand, had a problem of smaller dimension, but no less puzzling. Drawing employees from 216 towns and villages in the five boroughs of New York, Nassau and Suffolk Counties, they were acutely sensitive to the need to maintain wholesome community relations. This is not easy for a defense industry which must endure the feast or famine see-sawing typical of the business, each oscillation triggering economic upheavals due to extensive hiring or widespread layoffs. Before mounting a massive community relations program, Republic's president Mundy I. Peale reasoned that it would be wise to get a more precise reading on just what the public's attitude toward the company was. As a result, independent surveys were taken in a representative sampling of the communities from which the company drew employees. They discovered, for example, that while three out of four Long Islanders like Republic, few were aware of its charitable contributions, its support of civic groups, its sponsorship of youth activities and the like. Further, while they didn't blame the company directory for layoffs, they were unaware that it had to compete for business like any other commercial firm. They thought defense contracts were parceled out along political lines. Findings such as these helped shape the company's community relations program. They led to programs like a Community Days open house weekend which drew 135,000 neighbors to the plant, a 50-man speaker's bureau that addressed 70 organizations covering 4,900 people, involved nearly 2,000 Long Islanders on plant tours, and sponsored a special news digest film that was used by 94 schools with a monthly audience of 80,000.

Earlier, when the company was instituting a transfer of employee records to IBM cards, public relations requested that data on extracurricular activities be included as standard information. As a result, when attention was directed to community relations, it was a relatively simple matter to conduct an audit of employee activity. Tabulating results from 4,900 cards out of 6,200 non-bargaining unit employees' cards pulled showed that excellent material for stories, articles and photos resulted from this analysis.

Category	Membership	Employee Officers
Charities	1208	168
Youth groups	1083	396
Community activities	131	32
Civic organizations	1575	119
Government	351	41
Military organizations	346	63
Professional groups	827	53
Other activities	463	119
TOTALS	5984	891

Hugh Hoffman is president of Opinion Research Corporation, which over the past 10 years has probably done more probing of the corporate psyche and the id and ego of its neighbors than any other firm. He says that its file of some 1500 to 2000 corporate case histories covers the spectrum of questions a company would like to know the answers to. For example, it's done considerable work helping companies decide on a name change, with some dramatically different results. In another, a merger was found to have drastically reduced public familiarity with the name of the combined organization. In a third case, ORC worked with a company to pre-check a proposed name change; found that it would have been a bad strategic move, and dropped the idea.

The corporate image has come in for analysis, too. ORC has worked with companies to identify weaknesses or soft spots in the company's reputation, as well as to devise scientifically-based strategies to build familiarity with either the general public or special publics. In one instance, a company increased its public familiarity twenty points in less than two years through the simple expedient of identifying the company with its better-known consumer product names. A reputation among security analysts for "thinness at top" was uncovered on behalf of another company and remedial measures taken. It was successful to the point that this same company is now characterized as having the "outstanding management in its industry," primarily because of its management depth.

For another thing, you will find that executives who regularly defer to one another's particular specialty (i.e., sales, engineering, production) instinctively become "experts" in public relations. Each has firm and usually differing views on how this new management "tool" should be applied. The call for a corporate Solomon has to be answered by the chief executive officer because he must also be the chief executive officer of public relations policy. His is the broadest, least parochial view. His actions, philosophies and attitudes set the

31

tone and the pace of the company, and no activity is more responsive to these than public relations. This decision may come easily; more likely than not the public relations director will have to force such formal action into being. Difficult or easy, it is fundamentally *his* responsibility to get this mandate. Indeed, his first major contribution can come from being the catalyst in prompting the enterprise to identify, for perhaps the first time, just precisely what its goals are and how the public relations program can become related to these ends.

For practical purposes the objectives, or goals, should be specific rather than general. You should steer clear of accepting any of the wide screen, umbrella-like ambitions that are difficult to grapple with. For instance, it makes better business sense to mount a program calculated to improve the company's reputation or identity in a new or existing field than it is to broadly suggest the program's design to: "improve the company's image." Ask: "What image? Where? What's wrong with our existing one? When should this be done?"

THREE THUMBNAIL PROFILES

When Honeywell made its initial entry into the computer arena it created a new company, Datamatic Corporation, sharing parenthood with Raytheon. Its public relations objectives were short and precise. One, "to develop recognition for the (new) company as a major factor in electronic data processing." Two, to "stimulate respect for the resources, both technological and physical, inherent in the firm and its product." Three, "to build a reputation for Datamatic with actual and potential customers." This was further translated into a 1,400-word outline that pinpointed external and internal programs, detailed four major initial targets and gave a sense of the day-by-day activity by recommending ten immediate activities oriented to external publics and five directed internally. All of this was pegged to a specific timetable.

32

A 31-page program analysis and recommendations for Republic Aviation opened with five specific public relations objectives. One, "to report and reiterate the technological expansion and new capabilities of the company." Two, "to emphasize the financial soundness of the company." Three, "to find ways to dramatize the mission of the F-105." Four, "to improve impressions of corporate management and to introduce the new sales and engineering heads." Five, "to restore community confidence in the company's future."

Similarly, a recent public relations program for Bulova Watch Company was built around five objectives. Each was prefaced with analysis of where the company stood, the status of recent activity in the particular area and a rationale for the recommendations to follow. Covered were such areas as the company itself, which had then achieved the apex of an internal/external renaissance; its investor relations or financial community posture; consumer and product promotion; its relationships with its own industry and with its employees. A program of at least six months of detailed activity in support of these various objectives was spelled out, and areas of responsibility of the four-man staff were charted in detail.

None of these programs are exceptional. Any professional could develop, and regularly does develop, similar ones for his company.

The meticulousness of the programming, or its creative content, does not, of course, assure results. But it increases the chances by great odds.

Without a blueprint such as this, almost any public relations director will be hard pressed to rise above the minutiae that daily threaten to bury him. Nor will he, as a consequence, be able to generate the unstinting company-wide support that any program of significant magnitude demands. Busy people have little empathy with managers who can't be specific about their operations. They want to know what he wants from them, what he'll use this input for and, finally, what it can do for them.

PRIORITY AND DISCIPLINE—
KEYS TO PROGRAMMING

Because public relations is still, apparently, immunized from the conventional arithmetic of work measurement and disciplines (i.e., X hours vs daily or weekly results), it is generally beyond the ken of most businessmen to know whether busyness on the part of their public relations expert is related to results. Or is he just generating a smokescreen?

For their own part, many public relations people themselves scarcely know the distinction. Too regularly they succumb to the occupational euphoria characteristic of their trade, and equate human strain and dedication with professional effectiveness. This Hardy-boy attitude, however refreshing it may be today in an increasingly cynical world, does not make for professionalism or efficiency any more than a course in first aid makes a surgeon.

Assuming the professional experience that supports judgment, the top grade public relations man has two other basic ingredients: he knows *what comes first* and he has the *guts* to stick to his course.

You may encounter this attitude, so you'd better understand it.

A public relations man without a sense of priority is rudderless. Common sense dictates that any program must have realistic, achievable goals. Public relations often is a matter of opportunism, so one has got to be flexible. But over the long pull, the public relations adviser knows that the program he's presented, and which management has studied and approved, points to precisely the results they are expecting. However many times you may disturb his orderly execution of this program with spontaneous assignments, your evaluation of his success will still largely be based on how much of this he performs and how well—and he knows it and refuses to be seduced into thinking that the peripheral projects substitute for the original goals.

34

The guts come in when the pressure to take these side excursions grows—the meetings that are musts; the personnel manager who needs a hand in improving his plant newspaper; the sales manager whose reheated product has not responded to advertising resuscitation and who's looking to public relations for a last-ditch restorative. Both priority and discipline suggest the answer.

The choice isn't always so obvious. Often the spontaneity of sudden projects is immensely more appealing than the drudgery of programmed commitments. The confident (as well as competent) public relations man will rely on his judgment to juggle the mix of assignments so that his eye is never really taken off the main goals.

It is obvious that the public relations program must respond to some timetable; realistically this must be one that is oriented to the basic objectives of the corporation. Whatever the time period involved (daily, weekly or monthly), a determined effort should be made to spread creative time over many areas. A typical time allocation might run as follows:

TYPICAL TIME ALLOCATIONS

Activity Area	Time to Be Spent
Corporate (financial, general policy; corporate identity)	50%
Sales Support/consumer (market leadership; product publicity; trade communication)	25%
Technical (engineering; professional areas)	15%
Optional or Secondary Corporate (community, employees, plant communication)	10%
	100%

35

This budget suggests only an approach. How much is invested in each particular area is, of course, determined differently by different companies. But without a guide the public relations operation, be it one-man or a staff, will lack the diversification that it can and should bring to the company. Perhaps the informal character of public relations in general creates the need, but it is a fact that the most successful experts in this field work against some fixed, written and generally irrevocable yardsticks. It is a practical hedge against wasted time.

Maybe you never thought about it much, but there are fewer working days in a year to accomplish results than most programs reflect. First of all the public relations man doesn't have 365 days but, on the average, only 260 working days. Subtract at least ten days for vacation time and, in the public relations area, a month for the annual report chore, and he's down to about 210 days. Add in at least another month of time invested in "other" corporate priorities and he comes up with some 180 days free for pursuits of his listed objectives, free of interference and disruptions. So, he works weekends and holidays to gain some extra hours. But the fact remains that the time available for developing his program runs about half of the calendar year.

Bear this in mind when reviewing the program. Above all it must be realistic. Public relations people are sometimes carried away with naïve zeal.

What do you look for in a program? How definitive could *you* be about a neighboring company's sales program, or its marketing or engineering schedule? It's no less difficult to suggest an all-purpose formula for public relations. Naturally, there are fundamental bases to be touched. For example, by priority and subject content, any program that includes the following elements is moving in the right direction:

TYPICAL ASSIGNMENT PRIORITIES

Primary	*Secondary*	*Optionals*

Financial
   investor relations
   annual report;
     interim reports
   annual meeting
   analyst
     communication
	New product
	 development
	
	 Sales policy
	   industry speeches
	   market analysis
	   trend stories
		Appointments,
		 product changes to
		 trade
		
		 Trade/industry talks,
		 chapter level
		
		 Goodwill employee/
		 community liaison

Corporate
 developments
   acquisitions
   product
     breakthrough
   capital investment
   major addresses
   major executive
     appointments
   board actions
	Appointments—
	 trade/industry
	
	 Sales training
	
	 Trade show/
	 convention support
	
	 Special events
	 support
	
	 Plant/employee
	 communication
		House organ
		 supervision
		
		 Brochure copy

Broad employee/ labor developments		
Major community relations		
Research achievement		
Management corporate/ identification		

TO DISPENSE WITH A FEW SHIBBOLETHS

There is obviously more to assay in any public relations program than its weight in detail, organization and rhetoric.

37

Some of your own reactions will be instinctive and intuitively correct. Still, you may profit from some candor based on nearly twenty years of developing and presenting such programs to management.

FIRST, be suspicious of any program that seems to place the weight of action solely on activities and policy actions that the company is obliged to take first. I've said that public relations has no business endorsing the status quo, and this is no contradiction. But change generally has to be evolutionary, not an overnight coup. Public relations cannot cop-out on its responsibility simply because management didn't move as it so wisely and no doubt pontificately suggested. It has to work first with what currently exists, and rare is the company that does not have ingredients that can be translated into some kind of positive public relations programming.

SECOND, the reverse is also true; namely, be worried about the program that dedicates itself only to that which exists but suggests no new inputs, has no criticism of some actions or policies, and appears content to stir around in the existing environment without challenge. Corporate publicity, especially if you've never had much of it before, can be a heady experience but, like a skyrocket, it's forgotten in a flash and is misleading in terms of measuring success of any program.

If you need a specific yardstick, look for at least 50 per cent creativity in your program. Some 25 per cent of the activity can be expected to be built around events and happenings traditional with the corporation (i.e., open houses, annual meetings, sales meetings, etc.). The remaining quarter originates within the resources of the company, the result of screenings, story and project inventories, etc., by the public relations staff.

THIRD, and, finally, I'd say worry about the mettle of the public relations adviser who capitulates too quickly under fire and lacks the iron to articulately defend his proposed program. If he's any good, he's going to suggest something—

38

projects or activities—that, at first blush, you may find difficult to appreciate. Maybe you haven't the least bit of interest in having a community open house; perhaps you can't see why it's any reporter's business to know how much such-and-such a product line generates in income. You may be right. But then, you don't need a high-priced, talented public relations man on hand simply to agree with you, do you? Yes-men come a lot cheaper.

Listen to your public relations man's arguments; over-rule him if necessary, *but reflect* on how he conducted himself. Did he persist too long? Did he give up too fast? Did he do his homework and have facts and figures? Or did he simply expect you to accept his word for it?

This may be the most difficult time of all for you to be objective, because you will be emotionally involved. If you're challenged with some firmness and logic, you've probably got a good man.

CHAPTER FOUR

What Does It Cost
(Realistic Budgeting)

How much does a public relations program cost? What is reasonable? What is inflationary? This is no more an exact science than determining what is the "proper" advertising budget. A modest $50,000 might be adequate, or $1,000,000 could be required to cover all the bases without any frills or fat. So you won't get too much insight by investigating what others are investing in this area, unless you can find a company that's a carbon copy of yours, with not only the same sales and earnings but with similar objectives, and goals.

The public relations budget is sensitive to fiscal restraints. Yet, it is a mirror of the company's character and its ambitions. And this is as individualistic as the people running the show.

Obviously the more areas and more responsibilities a public relations program encompasses, the more it is going to cost. You need no special ability to weigh the appropriateness of overhead expenses and most general administrative costs inherent in conducting any such program. But you may have some difficulty in judging personnel requirements, both in salary range and in number, as well as such other appropriations as those for communications tools, films, tapes, mats, outside creative services, and the like.

40

What Does It Cost (*Realistic Budgeting*)

First, however, a few general guidelines:

Point one, don't hobble a skilled public relations man with a tight, inflexible budget and/or a tiny budget. The best engineer or advertising director would be helpless without a reasonable operating budget; public relations offers no secret formula to overcome such a hurdle. Money alone is not the answer, of course. Perhaps nowhere is there more imprudent investment of public relations dollars than in our universities and colleges, a segment of our society not known for its affluence. A poll by Hofstra University of some 36 universities disclosed public relations budgets ranging from $25,000 to over $678,000 with staffs from one to thirty. But despite these sizeable allocations, the universities were not getting fair returns on their investments because, by and large, the moneys were being spent on canned communications, in publications and in such periodicals as alumni news bulletins which have minimal impact or public relations value. So, dollars alone will not achieve the results you want.

Point two, don't inundate your public relations department with a pile of corporate courtesy assignments (garden club notices for the wife; executive articles for college alumni magazines) unless you have provided staff enough to absorb these time-consuming low-priority chores.

Point three, accept the fact that any sound public relations program must be founded in consistency. Effective communication with a few or a wide range of publics important to the company must be done with regularity. The creativity and volume requisite to this cannot be generated by a one-man staff.

Since cost is a product of the organization, it will help take some of the uncertainty out of this to consider a basic departmental setup. Primarily, of course, your concern will be economic, but you should have some idea of the building blocks that lead to that. We're arbitrarily excluding the one- and two-man staff operations; they're not really pertinent and represent either a high degree of improvisation, a low echelon

41

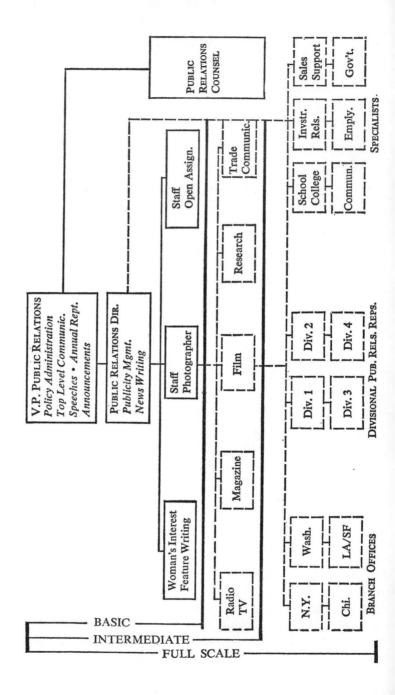

post or what usually amounts to private and exclusive counsel to the president.

At the top of the *basic* structure you'll have a vice president for public relations; he concerns himself with policy, administration, top level creativity (annual report, speeches, major pronouncements). His immediate aide is the public relations director or the publicity manager. His activities center on general communication, newswriting, publicity scheduling, special events handling, etc. Backing them up are, minimally, three other staff assistants: a women's writer who doubles as a feature writer; a chief photographer (a public relations department without top-level visual capability is obsolete) and a staff writer who works on creative writing across the board.

This is a tight department, and within its geographic restrictions (one office location) it can do a creditable job for an aggressive company in the $50 million to $100 million annual sales range. The department budget for such a five-man staff (including clerical and secretarial) would run about $100,000, with some 40 to 60 per cent devoted to salaries.

An *intermediate size* organization would probably add media experts in radio and television, magazines, film, research and trade communications. The mix may vary from company to company, but generally the growth or expansion of public relations departments is in the form of beefing up of staff expertise. Again, while salaries will constitute the bulk of the increased budget appropriation, there will also be a corollary facilities-costs increase. These additional staff experts will generate a higher volume of activity, which will boost all variable expenses to a higher level (stationery, travel, telephone and telegraph, entertainment, postage, etc.).

A rule-of-thumb measure is that each experienced staffer will create an average of $2000 to $3000 extra in operating costs over and above his own salary. In other words, a $15,000 staff member will represent an $18,000 budget entry.

A *full-scale* all-encompassing program would justify

43

USE OF THE PUBLIC RELATIONS DOLLAR

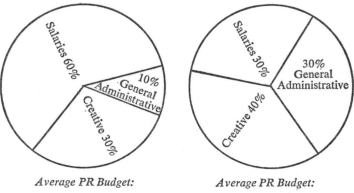

Average PR Budget:
$150,000-$200,000

Average PR Budget:
$1,000,000-plus

additional staff members and experts to devote almost full time to major segments of the publics of critical importance to the company. Major divisions or plants would probably require resident public relations support, with coordination and policy direction emanating from headquarters. It is also generally considered to be of strategic importance to have media liaison representation at key geographic communication relay points. These include New York, Chicago, Washington and Los Angeles or San Francisco. If the company has offices or major units in these cities, it obviates the need for special representation.

Departmental organizations such as this run at the top of the scale, in the $250,000-and-up category. They're not unusual, as a poll of some 166 companies by the Public Relations Society of America found in a 1960 survey.

A representative example of a million-dollar public relations department operation is that of New York's Chase Manhattan Bank. It's headed by a vice president, who reports to an executive vice president. A staff of 58 reports to the public relations v-p. There are 24 professionals, 21 special staff personnel (including tour guides) and 13 clerical workers. The staff is divided into six major groups, all of whose chiefs report directly to the assistant public relations director. These major units are news bureau (16 staffers), community relations (18), public affairs (4), editorial services (5), special events and services (5) and international public relations (4). This organization—obviously one of the best and certainly the most extensive—reflects the philosophy of president David Rockefeller. He believes that banks "must act so as to assure public acceptance of their practices and policies . . . (or they may) find their activities will be so circumscribed as to make them ineffective in their commercial role."

COMPANIES REPORTING ANNUAL SALES AND THE SIZES OF THEIR PUBLIC RELATIONS BUDGETS

Annual Sales	Total No. Amer.	New Eng.	Mid. Atl.	South	Mid-west	Far West	Can-ada
Under $50M	$75M	$56M	$85M	*	$80M	*	$60M
$51–100M	80M	75M	100M	80M	*	80M	70M
$101–200M	150M	140M	163M	*	151M	143M	143M
$201–300M	125M	*	138M	120M	125M	*	*
$301–500M	250M	*	280M	*	262M	*	*
$500–1000M	550M	*	660M	*	*	*	*

* Insufficient replies for a fair evaluation separately. (Copyright *PR Reporter,* 1968.)

Costs—always a controlling factor—may inhibit full execution of any of these three fundamental organizational structures. Rather than compromise on objectives, manage-

INTERNAL PUBLIC RELATIONS ORGANIZATION

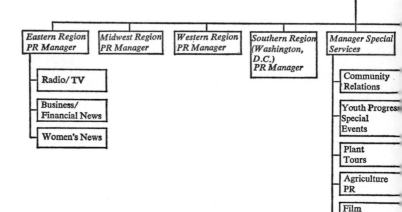

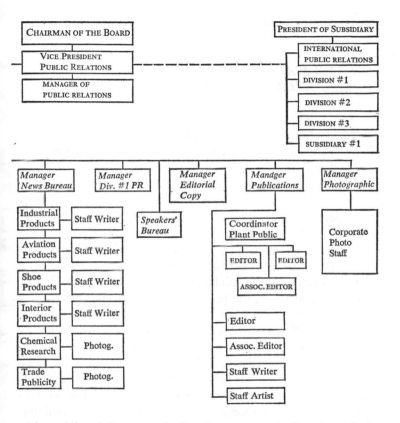

The public relations organization for a corporate department budgeting $2 million is illustrated here. This organization chart, representing, with minor changes, the structure of a company ranking among the top 25 of *Fortune's* 500 largest corporations, reflects both the diversity and the professional management control of the corporation itself.

ment has another option to consider. And that is to retain outside public relations counsel to provide the necessary manpower and brainpower to handle the assignment.

ON THE MATTER OF PUBLIC RELATIONS COUNSEL

A word here on the advantage, creatively and economically, of obtaining the services of counsel.

The question is fairly asked, "what does public relations counsel offer that we cannot provide in-house?"

Initially, consider the intangibles—the creative aspects.

In the full sense, public relations counsel offers a level or a degree of professional service that is generally hard for management to match, at comparable costs. It offers specially trained and experienced people who can diagnose management problems in the public relations areas, recommend solutions or means for minimizing such problems and, finally, but of pivotal value, the resources to *implement* change.

Outside counsel has many values beyond the base merits of economy. Some of these are hard to measure by traditional accounting yardsticks or pragmatic business judgments. For example, take objectivity. This is the prime and basic value you get from an outside service agency, be it public relations, advertising or management counseling. To agree is akin to voting in favor of motherhood; of course, a free and untrammeled mind is expected, you say.

But maybe your internal corporate environment strongly favors keeping even this function "within the family."

Outside counsel, as a service agency that daily must justify its paycheck, has stronger motivation to objectivity. There is no substitute for the independent, impartial and fresh viewpoint it generally represents. It's free from the personal interests, internal loyalties or company tradition that color too many corporate staff decisions. A strong sense of internal survival can weaken one's resolve.

But there are more things than judgment and backbone that you buy with a consultant. Obviously you'd expect broad experience. An additional advantage is analytical skill—the kind of specialist's detached intuition that cuts to the marrow of the problem and uncompromisingly suggests an avenue of, if not escape, certainly of graceful exit.

And finally—but by no means the least of the assets you contract for with a competent, all-around public relations consultant—the means and resources to execute the courses of action suggested. In a sense, this is the moment of truth: there can be a degree of arrogance in public relations pontification that can be justified only by doing—by accomplishment. Some counseling firms commit themselves to advise only *if* they can have a major hand in the final product, the action taken. The reason is obvious; even the best idea or advice can be bungled in the execution.

It's usually cheaper to use outside counsel, if you try to maintain a multi-city public relations operation. The fixed overhead costs of your internal staff almost surely would far outrun the per diem charges made by many of the counseling firms.

Two intangibles enter here for consideration. One concerns value; the other, judgment vs folklore.

Consider the first. The representative of the public relations counseling firm is usually an agent for more than one commercial interest. As such he has proportionately more to offer—in the way of information service—to the news media with which he must work, than the one-dimensional company representative. After all, how many major news stories can *one* company break in a month? Multiply that number by three or thirty and the more universal appeal of the counsel representative is apparent. "But," you say, "no one can know our company as our own people do." True, a

49

strong point in favor of company representation. But the outsider will normally be better versed in the subtleties of the problem to be faced, because no doubt he has been over similar ground many times in the past.

George Hammond avers public relations is essentially a probationer's business, an art of management counseling that transcends any body of knowledge and mechanical skills the consultant—be he internal or external—possesses. One learns by the hard lessons of experience; and it figures that a consultant will have *more* exposure to *more kinds* of problems than the corporate public relations man who probably has worked his way up the ladder in a company.

HOW DO YOU MEASURE CREATIVITY— WHAT'S IT WORTH

Assuming that an enlightened view has carried you this far, and you're willing to maintain an open mind on this matter of budgets, what tip can we provide that will give you the additional insights you seek? What, for example, is creativity worth? We'll not pretend to offer what older and wiser experts have not yet deemed it prudent to provide. But, with that *caveat,* let's see how close we can get to sketching some guidelines.

It all boils down to a matter of policy—and policing.

Before you set policy on this, don't try to equate results or even performance with the role of the press release. This is a golden myth some people hold of public relations impact, to wit: a segment of the public misunderstands you, so you inundate them with the proper information (i.e., press releases) *ergo,* they are converted! Would that it were that simple, but, obviously, it's not.

Generally what the public relations man is dealing with is not so much an unfriendly audience, as an obstinate one.

What Does It Cost (Realistic Budgeting)

Social scientist W. Phillips Davison points out that the audience is not a passive recipient. It can't realistically be regarded as a lump of clay, to be molded by the master propagandist. It's an audience made up of individuals who demand something from the communications they are exposed to. They select those that are likely to be useful to them. In other words, if you want to get something from them, they have to get something from you. A bargain is involved. And make no mistake, the audience can drive a hard bargain.

And that is why it is futile to try to apply customary criteria of job-and-recompense measurement to the public relations arena. How do you cost out your public relations director's ability to cope with the delicacy and complexity of this relationship between audience and communicator? It can't be measured on a time clock.

Results are, of course, the ultimate measure. But remember that these do not necessarily yield to the timetable of quotas and annual performance. To try to force this kind of meterage on public relations activity or output invalidates the very mission you've commissioned your expert for. That being to make lasting improvements, not crash programs of communication first aid.

There is no classical way to translate eight hours of applied creativity into a hard and fast balance sheet entry. Charlie may spend 60 per cent of the time listening and thinking, whereas Peter, an activist, reverses it and concentrates on tangible activity. Who's worth more? Only time and performance will tell. The public relations department spends several months working on the annual report. The accounting department sniffs, "All they did was write 20 pages . . . we gave them all the information . . . we could've done the job ourselves if we'd had the time."

But you're not weighing the pages, counting the words or tallying up the days involved. You're judging whether or not the report gives the company's owners a true perspective

51

on the activities of several thousand people over the long pull of a year's operation. Does the report communicate confidence, accomplishment, capability? Do you really think accountants, addicted to their stylized, cold-blooded idioms could have done the job?

So much for the philosophy of policy. Contrary to an impression that might have been given earlier, there are some practical areas for policing creativity—especially at the staff level. Forecasts of monthly work assignments, followed up by weekly work report summaries, themselves based on daily time sheet entries, take much of the mystery and most of the casualness out of public relations operations.

This does not mean that one story is calculated to be worth four hours of time, two stories at eight hours, etc. It can't be that inflexible. But the public relations director knows that a month of 20 working days will have 140 productive hours per staffer (7 hours per day), whereas a month of 22 working days will have 154 productive hours. Against this potential he usually applies his own rule-of-thumb yardstick for matching output to wool-gathering. The discipline of weekly reporting on activity or accomplishment for a five-day span is usually enough to guarantee reasonable levels of daily conscientiousness.

Since many public relations departments charge off some portions of the overhead costs to major company divisions, it is important to determine what share of the public relations effort they are getting, over and above that which accrues to them as part of the corporate benefits. One method is to have staff members log project time; this gives a quick summary comparison at the month's end.

Even when such time is not billable to the divisions involved, such a detailed analysis provides the department's administrator with a statistical picture of how time is being spent on what activities, etc. Corrective action, if required, then becomes a matter of routine.

What Does It Cost (*Realistic Budgeting*)

WORK ANALYSIS SHEET

REPORT OF...

Project Assignment	Activity	Distribution of Time by Days 1 2 3 4 5 6 7 8 9 10 11 12 13 14 15 16 17 18 19 20 21 22 23 24 25 26 27 28 29 30 31							Total Hours	Cost	
		Grand Total										

.... Week Ending.................... 196..................... ....
Approved   signed

A FINAL—AND PERSONAL NOTE

Before you plunge into a disgruntled criticism of your public relations adviser's daily work habits ("he never seems to be busy; he's always talking to, or visiting with, somebody"), take a look at your own day. Unless you are an extraordinary executive, you waste time yourself to an appalling degree. At least that's what a study of the work habits of 179 board chairmen and presidents by a Chicago management consulting firm recently revealed. It showed that the typical American executive, in a 12½-hour day, gets only an average of two hours alone, and even this is crowded with backlogged memos, letters and reading matter. The thinking and planning that lie at the heart of the chief executive officer's job get the lowest priority. The surveyors, Daniel D. Howard and Associates, not unnaturally conclude that only a small percentage of the firms—about 28 per cent—are getting full returns on their investment in their chief executive officers. A secondary conclusion is that the boss is letting others control and waste his time.

'Nuff said?

WHAT IT ALL ADDS UP TO

Totaling this all up—the scope of the objectives, the breadth of the organization, the common denominators of expense, the unyielding informality of the art, and the often enigmatic rationale of the audiences with which it must cope—reinforces the point made earlier in the chapter: it's not so much a question of how much it costs, but rather, one of how much you want to accomplish.

CHAPTER FIVE

Public Relations vs Advertising

The title of this chapter simply recognizes a worn and fading contest. Actually the presumed antagonism between these two creative, imaginative disciplines has always been a synthetic one. Basically, there is no conflict. They should never be in competition for the same corporate dollar.

To function without either a formal public relations program or an advertising campaign, using, instead, a jerry-built amalgam of the two, is akin to competing with half your sales staff on vacation; to employ both skills, but in an atmosphere of survival competition, is simply an acute case of corporate short-sightedness, from which, it might be added, the company may never fully recover.

These two resources—however different and special their techniques, applications and even their philosophies— are as interdependent as Siamese twins. They are two sides of the same coin, and those who direct each should work in close harmony, if not hand-in-hand.

But if there's one element that makes corporations unpredictable and their activities less than exact, it is that they are still run by people, not computers. The logic of the marriage between advertising and public relations is often lost on the participants, who are also immune to shot-gun wedlock. Realistically, therefore, the basic differences in style, technique, attitude and, principally, in responsibility still need to be detailed.

A flip definition says that advertising sells products while public relations sells the company. Of course, but like so many shorthand descriptions, it leaves unsaid more than it says. What about institutional advertising, or public service advertising? They sell the company, generally, more than they sell products. Conversely, no publicist will say that product publicity campaigns don't sell products, or that application stories have any other purpose. There's obviously a generous cross-over to the point sometimes where it seems that the advertising operators are moving into public relations problems and that the public relations men are edging into the marketer's province. Actually, there is nothing fundamentally wrong in this crossing over, if it's coordinated and under control.

To help get this whole matter into focus, we begin by debunking one enduring myth. Advertising is not simply salesmanship in print; it does not sell products, per se. Adman Fairfax Cone got to the marrow of the situation, exposing the advertising vs public relations controversy for what it really is, by pointing out that they both promote the company and/or the products, and he even defied anyone to measure which did the better job. Furthermore he had the audacity to suggest that the public relations experts, who usually must stick scrupulously to the facts, might help advertising men, who are generally expected to demonstrate a certain amount of unbridled exaggeration, by dissuading their clients from inviting such excesses in the first place.

Cone's statesmanship is an uncommon quality on either side of this communications avenue. Consequently, the controversy persists. Some of the sharp edges can be removed if advertising is viewed in the broader context of being part of the total marketing effort of the company.

To do that we must ask again, "Why do companies

56

advertise?" That may seem like a monumentally stupid question. The answer is obviously: to sell products—no matter how you slice the rationalization. Curiously, though, increasing numbers of advertising experts are candidly admitting that advertising cannot actually sell goods. It can do little more than inform the consumer about a product and perhaps excite his curiosity about it. Supporting this unusual thesis, the Association of National Advertisers defined advertising as "mass, paid communication, the ultimate purpose of which is to impart information, develop attitude and induce action beneficial to the advertiser" (logically, the sale of a product or service). The Association emphasized that advertising was just one in a series of tools in what it called the "marketing-communications mix." The other tools were identified as person-to-person selling, retailer recommendations, publicity, special promotions and so on. Ostensibly, advertising's job is to perform certain aspects of the communicating job with greater speed and volume than can be accomplished by any other means.

This wide-screen view is not restricted to institutional or public service advertising, either. It applies specifically and directly to product advertising. A contemporary of Cone's— Walter Weir, adman, executive and author—says that product advertising, by the manner in which it is addressed to the reader, can strongly influence the "image" the public develops of the company sponsoring the product. In turn, this affects the public's attitude toward the product itself, the company's stock, its management and its future.

Instinctively, one thinks of some outlandish, tasteless ads and wonders what havoc they must wreak on corporate images. Ad experts refuse to acknowledge that advertising ever consistently annoys the reader. Weir insists that no company would long tolerate a salesman who regularly annoys the people on whom he calls, no matter how successful he is in selling the product. To his side marches Paul Foley,

57

president and board chairman of McCann-Erickson, who says that selling cannot be done by denigration and irritation. Longevity is proof that ads, no matter how far out they may appear, are successful, because they appeal to someone.

Time, gentlemen! We'll not extend the misunderstanding by pointing out several instances of apparent corporate myopia on this score. The point made is nevertheless valid, to wit: It is incorrect, impractical (and shortsighted) to think of advertising solely in terms of product advertising, since the sum of its effects can be so far-reaching.

Even the most vigorous disciple of either talent must recognize these truths: The purchase of products is influenced by a host of personal, social and environmental factors not necessarily responsive to the strongest advertising or sales effort. Similarly, any sound, sophisticated program conceived to improve the rapport between a company and any of the publics affecting its ability to grow and conduct its business profitably cannot exclude any proven avenue or medium of communication—certainly not advertising.

One measure, therefore, of your public relations man's competence and professional maturity will be in his approach to and his attitude toward this relationship, his empathy, the spirit with which he collaborates, philosophically and otherwise, with his advertising and marketing contemporaries.

His attitude—assuming it to be enlightened—will, of course, be only as effective as the support you give him. Unless you've been through this mill, you can anticipate debate over budgets, planning and strategy of control of territorial prerogatives, and, of course, ego clashes. There's no shortcut through this creative thicket short of executive edict, and that should be the last resort, since it only drives the disagreement underground.

Let's reverse normal procedures and look at the question of control last; the answer will suggest itself after analysis of the operational specifics.

THE BUDGET QUESTION

It's in the matter of budgets that harmony most often comes a cropper, especially when dollars are being set for a new product introduction. Nothing arouses the slumbering ambitions more, apparently, than contesting for that extra dollar. Should the $50,000 go for a new advertising program? Or should it go for a special grass-roots product publicity campaign? Each proponent champions his cause with vigor, logic, and a self-confidence guaranteed to overwhelm any but the most resolute arbiter.

The choice should not have to be made. If money's tight, most public relations budgets are flexible enough to absorb the extra work involved in the product publicity; in fact, provisions for such activity should have been anticipated and cranked-in earlier. At the same time, advertising budgets, although working on longer lead times and dollar commitments, have a degree of adaptability too, and dollars can often be found by reallocating some of those committed.

Essentially, however, the question should not really arise in the first place. There's no room for choice, any more than there is room for parochial egos. *Both* advertising and public relations should be employed. This is the only way to use the company's talent effectively. What sets one product campaign off from the next (and let's admit that few so-called new products are better mousetraps—most consist of new packaging, paint job and design more than anything else) is often the quality and the quantity of the publicity support behind it. (Chapter Seven substantiates this rather flat statement.) There's also an intangible plus in using both forces that's not usually acknowledged. It springs from the subtle impetus that wholesome competition builds between creative forces. This is not as Machiavellian as it sounds; creative people can be challenged, and by wiring both into a project,

59

with shared responsibilities, management stands a good chance of getting just a little bit more creative electricity flowing.

Before leaving product selling—or more properly, product educating—let's consider the relationship of public relations skills to sales promotion activities.

PUBLIC RELATIONS IN SALES PROMOTION STRATEGY

Even though the genesis for sales promotion traditionally rests in the advertising department, public relations can, and should be, an integral part of any such campaign. Public relations people, for example, are usually better versed in creating special events and projects that energize top notch sales promotion activities; they also give the communication phases greater believability, since letters, direct mail pieces, brochures, folders and other non-advertising techniques are utilized heavily. The advertising people, for their part, are better at graphics and sorts of peripheral support build-up via printed means. Visual media (TV) are natural to their arsenal, and they're ingenious in concocting themes, slogans and other catchy features that trigger public attention.

Each could cite dramatic examples of creative plums. But, limiting public relations examples to those of heavily editorial character, consider these:

An obsolescence campaign for Honeywell, conceived some years ago to underscore the need for modern home heating controls was supported by editorial material from its public relations department analyzing the ages of private homes and the various fixtures in the homes. Facts were assembled on a state-by-state basis. Newspaper and magazine stories reporting these findings, backed up by heavy radio commentary, highlighted the need for modernization of home heating and for temperature controls—and it scored the point in a way no paid-space printed message could do.

In another instance, Bulova Watch Company's public relations department organized city, state and regional week-long watch check-up periods, patterned after medical physical examinations. Objective: to demonstrate to people the inherent inaccuracy of their favorite timepieces, as a backdrop for a more conducive atmosphere for the company to sell its new, extraordinarily accurate electronic timepieces. The Correct Time Week promotions, officially proclaimed by Governors or Mayors in seven states, and supported by local civic clubs and neighborhood jewelers (who checked over the public's watches when they were brought in for examination), resulted in marked increases in sales of the timepiece, with increases ranging from 45 per cent in one city to 201 per cent in another.

In each case, advertising was a partner in the project; ads supported stories, and stories extended the theme and message as ads alone could not do. The tools public relations can bring to such promotional campaigns are impressive: films, speeches, stories, articles and photo spreads in local media; radio-TV appearances; interviews; often, full editorial support. The net effect of all of this was to generate word-of-mouth advertising, still the most direct communication of all. These are the ingredients that should be mixed into any well conceived promotional program.

A FEW WORDS ABOUT LETTERS

Next to talking, the most fundamental technique of person-to-person communication is, naturally, the letter. Letters are, of course, not exclusive to sales promotional programs; they permeate every phase of the company's communicating. But here is as good a place as any to introduce the subject, since direct mail (sometimes non-letters, unfortunately) is a main weapon of sales promotional activity.

Many public relations advisers, preoccupied with other,

headier forms of high-level communications strategy, delegate letter writing to the lowest staff member, or brush it off with hasty dictation. As a matter of fact, a survey of 15 public relations programs showed an impressive array of communication techniques—everything from closed-circuit television to corporate advertisements and elaborate booklets. Sadly, but not surprisingly, I found no specific attention given to the humble letter. Yet letters are and must be a key element in any comprehensive campaign to communicate anything.

A skillfully written letter is anything but ordinary. Writing letters is in fact dangerously self-deceptive. The writer is his own censor and the temptation to oversell is great. Enamored of his own words, the writer too quickly equates the deed with successful communication where in fact it may be accomplishing no such mission. Generally (Note: this *is* qualified), public relations people, by virtue of the daily catechism of skepticism encountered in dealing with media, are more practiced in the straight talk that makes an effective letter. Letters require at least as much objectivity and restraint as would be exercised in writing news stories. They also demand as much realism—the realism to ask oneself, who cares? Letters are less expensive than press releases (but barely; one letter costs an estimated $2.49 vs $1.00 to $2.50 for a page release) and thereby seem unworthy of a place in elaborate and expensive public relations budgets. But what kind of a campaign would it be that didn't use some of the following: letters to stockholders, to employees, to customers, to editors, to supervisors, to legislators, and to civic and community leaders? And then there's the host of "internal" letters, those vital intra- and inter-office memorandums that prop up modern business action.

The creative use of letters can be pivotal in promotional programs. For example, Bulova made a deliberate bid to stir rumors of its new electronic watch by having its president and the chairman of the board communicate directly, via letter, to 3,000 leaders in business, science, finance and government. They reported, with justifiable pride, their company's successful technical breakthrough in personal time-keeping. The recipients all accepted the letters in the spirit in which they were written. As a result of this nationwide letter-writing campaign, the company was assured that at least this important segment of opinion-molders was aware of its new product and its significance.

Still another unique use of letters to carry a message was one adopted by Republic Aviation Corporation. Its aim was to inform key elements of business, the government and the financial world that it was making a substantial corporate transition to the space age, as exemplified in the then forth-coming dedication of its new $14 million research and development center. To stimulate interest in this, the company asked pollster Elmo Roper and the Research Institute of America to develop an intriguing questionnaire on a variety of topics, soliciting opinions as to the status of these topics five years hence. The letter accompanying this poll, to 3,200 leaders in almost every field of achievement, explained that the advent of the research center's opening had stimulated this measurement of leadership opinion, etc. Once again, the letters and the poll (direct mail) carried the story of the research facility directly to those publics the company was keenly interested in.

CORPORATE ADVERTISING

A fast-growing manifestation of the corporate itch to communicate more thoroughly and expansively with its publics is the institutional or corporate advertisement. Some 700 American corporations and associations, at the latest count, invested $117 million in magazines alone in 1966 in corporate advertising. Ford led all with a $4.4 million expenditure, followed closely by General Motors, AT&T, General Telephone & Electronics, and General Electric. The top 50 companies alone (General Tire & Rubber, with a budget of $483,000, was 50th) spent $52.6 million in institutional advertising in such books as *Time, Business Week, Newsweek, Life, U.S. News & World Report, Look, Fortune, Reader's Digest, Forbes* and *Saturday Evening Post,* according to the rank reported by the Publisher's Information Bureau. (In 1967 the total outlay was $250 million.)

The broad scale diversification of companies, and the rise of the multi-product or multi-division conglomerates have no doubt added force to this mounting campaign in print. The corporate penchant for "doubling up" has almost quadrupled over the past few decades—1,496 mergers alone in 1967—and this has eroded the once-sharp distinction or image many companies could boast of.

There is a mushrooming need for telling how the new identities, trademarks or new capabilities resulting from mergers add up to increased customer or stockholder benefit in terms of products, services and technology. Communication of these new faces is a public relations assignment. In fact, it is the one specific advertising role public relations is charged with. The nub of these corporate advertising programs is not to sell products, but to communicate business philosophy, and this is a ticklish assignment, demanding keen appreciation of the intangibles that make up a corporate personality. The public relations expert may limit himself to translating the concept required to the company's creative advertising staff, or he may actually write the copy himself. Perhaps the most famous of all corporate advertising series was the pioneering campaign by Carl Byoir on behalf of The Great Atlantic & Pacific Tea Company, first in an institutional campaign that resulted in defeat of punitive anti-chain store taxation, and later to give the public A&P's side of the story in an anti-trust action brought by the federal government against the grocery chain. The A&P campaign against anti-chain legislation is still considered in public relations circles to be one of the outstanding accomplishments of the craft, for it is said that never before or since have so many people representing so many sectors of the American public appeared at congressional hearings as did in the program mustered to defeat the Patman anti-chain store act.

A survey of the motives of corporate advertisers in *Newsweek* magazine showed nine dominant themes:

Communication of identity and scope of the company.

Communicating expanded capabilities.

Communicating facilities and resources.

Communicating new products (to reflect creativity rather than to introduce the product).

Communicating new technologies (and commitment to long range growth).

Communicating foreign capabilities (trend toward multi-nationalism).

Communicating reputation and rewards (stimulate new talent).

Communicating growth and performance (stimulate investment).

Communicating interest and involvement (social responsibility, good citizen).

The sharp increase in corporate advertising places a heavier burden upon the creativity of public relations and advertising expert alike. A certain sameness has begun to permeate the advertising pages of *Business Week,* for example, where there's ample opportunity for side-by-side comparison of these institutional communications. The objectives are common, the graphics and technique almost homogeneous; only the ingredients differ, and even these differences sometimes seem minor, blending into a bland pattern. Hopefully, the skilled public relations man accustomed to coping with media initially indifferent to his efforts at communicating (he can't buy his way in; it's earned) will continue to demonstrate the same resourcefulness.

We turn, inevitably, to the matter of control, or of coordination. In short, who's boss?

COORDINATION'S THE KEY

It would be somewhat naïve to expect that ecumenicalism alone will build a smooth-functioning marketing/public relations team. Teamwork, or coordination, is not hereditary; it's a product of upbringing, of judgments and decisions.

Maybe, as Whit Hobbs, senior vice president of Benton & Bowles, once put it, public relations and advertising may not be legally married, but they "sure as hell have an arrangement." Whether they like it or not, they share the same customers, the same public. They're in the news business together; in the image-building business together and they need each other, even though, as Hobbs says, neither will admit it. Too often the right hand doesn't know what the left hand is up to, and both hands want it to be that way. A company must speak everywhere to everyone with one voice. Confusion and contradiction, says Hobbs, are costly and damaging. Obviously, therefore, someone has to set policy; someone has to have the over-all responsibility.

Who? Creative people worry a great deal over this status problem. Should control rest with the advertising or marketing executive? Or with the public relations vice president? Actually, the answer's as simple as the drive for status, manpower, larger budgets and management's attention make it complex. Control is a function of corporate policy, especially when viewing both skills in the broadest sense of total marketing. So, *QED*, control should be coordinated or centralized whereever policy is set.

Public relations is generally closest to management, cutting across all divisional lines to coordinate the company's total communications conduct. It is logical that it also embrace advertising, at least from the corporate policy point of view, to achieve effective coordination in planning and programming.

This does not mean that the public relations director

has to double as advertising manager. As a matter of fact that is *not* the best course. There are many techniques and deliberations peculiar to advertising that demand a specialist's direction as much as public relations needs commensurate professional experience. Daily responsibilities should be divided; the day-to-day functioning initiation and planning of the advertising department should be placed under supervision of its own departmental executive. Primary contact and responsibility will be with the sales department, as it should be. But over-all surveillance, for policy monitoring and to guard against the nuances that often can spell public relations trouble, inevitably rests with the top public relations executive.

What this seems to require is an administrator who is aware of the strengths and weaknesses of both creative fields and who shows partiality to neither. A public relations man of this stature is hard to find. Nevertheless, there is a marked trend in management circles to establish an office of public affairs, the executive in residence holding forth over both advertising and public relations. The rationale behind it reflects the most sophisticated approach: the responsibility for supervision of the company with all its publics, internal as well as those outside the family, logically requires the flexibility to utilize all resources pertinent to the job; any real coordination begins with authority broad enough to encompass *all* communications techniques.

At General Motors, which has one of the nation's most sophisticated public relations organizations (and product advertising, too, when it has institutional flavor), coordination of other advertising activity such as new model announcements and promotions is achieved at meetings of a personnel and public relations policy group which includes the vice president, marketing staff.

At giant American Telephone & Telegraph the public relations department is intimately involved in advertising. One of the four assistant vice presidents to the public relations vice president is responsible for advertising, principally print advertising, advertising in magazines and periodicals only; newspaper advertising is in the province of the associated companies where the local public relations executive is involved.

No inflexible yardstick can be set down for pinpointing the role of the public relations director in the total marketing picture. In smaller companies, or even in some larger ones just instituting public relations, the tendency is to incorporate both jobs in one, and give the public relations director responsibility for advertising as well. While management initially may find this acceptable, as the activity grows a natural separation will suggest itself. The public relations director will maintain, as we've seen the job emerge in the giant corporations, a strong influence on the marketing scene.

DON'T TRY TO DOUBLE UP

This partnership between advertising and public relations, which is growing daily as marketing itself becomes more complex, might suggest an expediency. To introduce public relations to a company lacking any such formal set up, why not utilize the existing public relations machinery of the company's advertising agency, or of an agency that combines both services? You can't call the rush of advertising agencies to offer public relations service a boom—one survey indicated that 45 per cent of the top agencies offered this service, as contrasted to 80 per cent only a decade ago. Nevertheless there are enough agencies around that offer public relations, in order to give a company a choice. Some agencies, especially where the public relations function rests in an affiliate or a subsidiary, will accept public relations accounts of companies, regardless of whether or not they handle the advertising business. Others, with internal public relations services, ordinarily serve only the needs of advertising clients. Whether or not you can find a home, the question is: "Is this the place for management to search for public relations assistance?"

The answer is "no!" This is admittedly a biased separation-of-church-and-state view, but with cause. Consider, first, the average agency's principal selling point: If management accepts the concept of total communication (a persuasive, ricocheting shot), then, the argument follows, isn't it logical to coordinate all the tools to do this in one shop? Isn't it bound to be more efficient, more economical and, hence, more businesslike?

Nope. For one thing, efficiency does not demand that all of the communications resources be grouped in one spot— any more than it would demand that your dentist be in the same building with doctors of the eyes, nose and throat, so that you could cover all your ills in one visit. The agency, even more than the internal advertising department, is basically preoccupied with selling products, of making the best use of dollars and media to reach the public. Granted some editorial competence to develop the product publicity to support the advertising campaigns, this is really thin qualification with which to tackle the larger, more encompassing responsibilities of public relations. It leaves uncovered, professionally, a wide range of responsibilities falling under the public relations mandate: employee and stockholder publications, annual reports, programs for government and community relations, technical news, youth activities, international relations, and so on.

Further, the essence of public relations service, to a company, is to be a professional listening post, to keep an ear on the public, and to suggest actions calculated to maintain a reasonable harmony. In some cases this action might be a non-action action; strategy might dictate keeping one's counsel and making no overt moves, as in a tight labor squabble; another time it might suggest stopping some action, i.e., an advertising campaign offensive to a particular group. An advertising agency, whatever its moral integrity, makes its money only on action; its entire modus operandi is dedicated to organization of ideas and programs that result in action—which is billable. In effect, an agency, for good, sound economic reasons, just does not have the options open to it that are necessary for public relations decision-making; nor does it have the depth of skills requisite for the diversified responsibilities involved in public relations.

To paraphrase the communications oracle and critic, Marshall McLuhan, the medium may be the message for advertising agencies; for public relations advisers, the message is the central thing. In other words, it's not by what means you say it, but what you say, itself; this is often the rudimentary difference in philosophy between the two skills.

CHAPTER SIX

Mirror on the Corporate Image

When the New York Yankees were winning pennants and world series with computer-like regularity—from the late '30s through the late '50s—and packing the stadium with 50,000 to 60,000 or more people per game, few would have imagined that a scant six years later, in 1965, they would be trying to lure customers in by offering free bats (or baseball hats) to youngsters, at the rate of 60,000 souvenirs a game.

What happened was that, once stripped of the godlike heroes that gave the club its sheen of invincibility—the Ruths, Gehrigs, Rolfes, Kellers, DiMaggios and Fords—its image as a cold, efficient baseball machine became plain for everyone to see. Baseball fans turned their backs on the Yankees, and went across the river to where the septuagenarian double-talker Casey Stengel and his bank of artless ball players enthralled and intrigued growing hordes of spectators, winning just often enough to preserve their Walter Mitty air. The New York Mets, as an expansion-created team, had no discernible image, so the inventive Stengel was able to sugarcoat their inelegant boggling. Conversely, the Yankees had an image that their proficiency had created for them, but it was the wrong one at the wrong time, so they're hard at work to erase that unfriendly façade.

Like the Yankees, many are concerned about images

71

these days—personalities, institutions, universities and, of course, companies. Richard Nixon worked hard to shed his image as a loser; the late Robert Kennedy, his image as a political opportunist; General Motors is trying to remove the splotches put on its corporate escutcheon by Ralph Nader; Dallas businessmen were asked to raise a $1½ million kitty for aid in improving the city's image; the pharmaceutical industry conducted a nationwide search for a new public relations executive with the creativity and energy to rebuild its public image, tarnished by coming out second best in a public wrangle with the Federal Food and Drug Administration. All of this raises these questions: "What is this business of image-making? What, in fact, is an image, corporate or otherwise? Why is it so important? Can it be created? Changed? Bought?

The corporate image—fourteen letters that spell out an alphabet of meaning and misunderstanding!

To some businessmen it's a panacea for all corporate ills, a magic communications elixir to whiten tattletale gray reputation. Others dismiss it as a fictitious creation of ingenious copywriters, inspired, no doubt, by the rewards in the form of advertising commissions. But it's fact, not fantasy, to hundreds if not thousands of companies who, not unlike the Yankees, grapple daily with the problem of getting the public to think of them as they would like to be thought of. Burnishing the corporate image is a full-time job. So you'd best understand what's involved and what your role is and realize that the responsibilities and commitments to this central task lie with your public relations department.

We begin with the word itself. It is characteristic of public relations that it is consistently burdened with terminology imposed on it by laymen. Image has no etymological roots in the practice of public relations; in fact, its application, as in image-building, is more brickbat than bouquet. The new Random House dictionary has 20 definitions of the word;

number 3 best reflects its use in public relations context. It defines image as, "a mental representation; idea; conception." It is what comes instantly to mind when you hear the name of a company if, of course, you've heard of it at all. In the strictest sense, therefore, every company can be said to have a corporate image. Every airline, every bank, every store, every manufacturer has a reputation, a personality, an identity that is associated with it. This is made up of many factors. The Twentieth Century all-Pullman train to Chicago projected associations of luxury, elegance in service, prestige, gourmet food and expense. Japanese products once symbolized copycat design, slipshod workmanship, cheapness. Today, this image—thanks to radical internal improvements—glistens with the fruits of technological and manufacturing innovation. While the image itself may be clear in a person's mind, the reasons he or she may give for holding such a view are based on vague generalizations. These hazy explanations cover, usually, a multitude of impressions and associations; nevertheless, these impressions make up the image to which everyone refers.

Perhaps the most definitive analysis of the corporate image, at least from a practical approach, was conducted by *Business Management* magazine. It sought opinions on the subject from a cross-section of public relations experts, advertising and graphic arts specialists, and a fair share of companies. In brief, the consensus was that the corporate image is two things. One, it is an impression that every corporation tries to convey through its advertising, public relations and other means. Two, it is the impression held by a vast array of individuals—the corporation's customer's, suppliers, and stockholders, to name a few of the obvious.

Such views will vary, of course, from group to group and from person to person within any one group. More important, the images held by the majority of these people may vary sharply with the image the company thinks it is projecting. The essence of public relations consists of bringing about a fair balance between these divergent views to minimize the distortions.

Is image-building, after all, just a fancy name for public relations work? Don't leap to conclusions. Public relations *is* involved, but the building of a reputation (née image-building) is not the exclusive province of any one communications skill. It is a part of every facet of the company's activity that involves communicating or dealing with people.

Granted, it's a glib term. Granted, it's a cliché. Granted, it is misused, abused and overused. Still, do not overlook its strategic importance as an operations tool. One industry observer, business journalist and analyst, Pierre Martineau, says flatly that the business executive cannot afford to scoff at this subject of images, because people are acting toward his company on the basis of them—not on the basis of facts and figures. He points out that once stereotyped notions are formed in people's minds they are extremely difficult to change. They serve as emotional filters that are used by everyone in listening and seeing. These images, he says, cause us to reject what we do not agree with while we allow agreeable material to pour in unchallenged. Thus the good image has a halo effect, so that the object "wearing" the halo gets credit for all sorts of good things.

Take one of the more pivotal arenas, the financial community. How does Wall Street weigh corporate worth? It's not all just a matter of arithmetic or economic scholarship. In a study of how the men of Wall Street rate the corporate image, it came out as something far from tangible. The report by an industrial design and marketing firm (Lippincott & Margulies) disclosed that corporate image was a big factor in investment selection. Because people are clearly influenced by the corporate image, the analyst must reckon with it, too. Concepts such as "aggressiveness in product research" (GE), "competence" (Procter & Gamble), "product and marketing excellence" (IBM), "technical com-

74

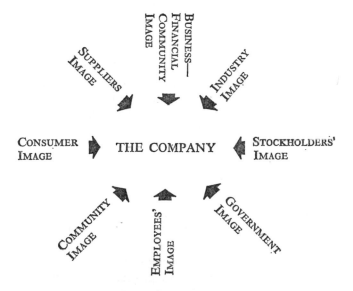

Corporate image in itself is a misnomer. Companies do not have single identities. Each group important to a company has its own perspectives, colored by individual viewpoints, attitudes and motivations. The sum of all of these is the mosaic that represents what is generally called the "corporate image," or reputation.

petence" (Polaroid), "innovator" (Control Data), were cited by the analysts as image attributes that merit consideration. Although they are intangibles they stem from something concrete. Accordingly, they become essential ingredients of investment analysis.

A poor corporate image ranked with lagging profits and the sagging price of the stock of General Dynamics Corporation as matters of concern to stockholders at the 1968 annual meeting. Stockholders urged the chairman and president, Roger Lewis, to strive, through publicity, to improve the company's image. Mr. Lewis said he recognized the need for an improved image and said that the matter was of high priority in the management.

And if the point needs further buttressing: Opinion Research Corporation, after ten years of studying corporate reputations in a systematic way, draws the conclusion from some 145,000 personal interviews that more and more companies are trading on their good reputations (corporate images) to help them meet specific corporate objectives by influencing people favorably.

HOW TO FOCUS THE IMAGE

Molding and shaping the corporate image demands a great deal of sophisticated know-how, dedication and enthusiasm. It requires more than the customary platitudinous advertising messages, dripping with syrupy expressions of good will. The practical way to project a clear persuasive corporate image begins in focusing on the corporation itself. Every activity of the enterprise adds some meaning to the public's picture of it. Nothing, of course, is perfect, but management and the public relations director may first have to face up frankly to several internal problems before any face-lifting is attempted. For example, if the company is saddled with a negative image (and here is where independent opinion research is a prime requisite) stemming from too-conservative policies, stodgy products and packaging, no amount of hoop-la will alter that basic fact. Cities Service changed its name to Citgo and launched its "Zoom" campaign, but its success was traceable to the fact that this activity was truly the external sign of major internal policy decisions to rejuvenate the company. The degree and depth of family house-cleaning needed will be a product of the survey. Not everything can be tidied up; the realistic public relations man knows that there are some things he'll just have to live with.

But at least his program will not contain any of the adolescent optimism or non-professional naïveté that surprisingly creeps into the planning of otherwise sane and sensible public relations advisers.

What can you, as management, expect from your public relations man in this area? Is overall image really his responsibility, since the result springs from a thousand decisions in the company and from the impact, good or bad, of a diversified array of products on a cross-section of the public? Can, indeed, anyone hope to coalesce all of these diverse "happenings" into a clear, understandable corporate image?

The answers are all affirmative.

Yes, it falls to the public relations director to assume this responsibility. He gets the mandate essentially because the corporate image is the product of such widely dispersed actions within the company. He is usually in the best central position to mobilize and synchronize all internal resources necessarily involved in the company-wide job.

The most direct and overt way, naturally, for the company to project its character to the public is by advertising. However, in the task of molding—developing is a more fitting term—a new image or personality there is an infinity of meanings and situations that cannot be approached by direct advertising. The format and tone of the annual report, the "cut of the jib" of the sales staff, the leadership and savoir faire demonstrated by executive management, the climate of the company environment, its participation in local and national problem-solving on social issues—these and countless other considerations just don't lend themselves to the functional dimensions of advertising.

The strategy of any communications program conceived to make measurable improvements in a company's reputation must be developed in the light of each firm's circumstances. Regardless of these variables, there is a fundamental program your public relations man will suggest.

77

THE BASIC FOUR STEPS

Any good reporter will turn in a story only if it answers five fundamental questions: "who," "what," "why," "where" and "when"? Such criteria can be applied just as effectively to the "tooling up" procedures for reputation renovating.

1. *Who are you now? What, really, does the company represent? Where is it going?* Before you can sensibly weigh the validity of your existing image, or make any logical suggestions for improvement, you must first determine the character of the company. Does it have a set of corporate objectives? Long range plans for its organized growth? If you can unearth them you may find the objectives interesting —probably out-of-date. The philosophical and judgmental exercise involved in updating them will be a healthful thing. For one thing, it precludes you and, in turn, your public relations adviser, from taking the company's course for granted. Anytime you challenge the status quo you're taking out insurance against unpreparedness. Over-confidence or smugness spells obsolescence in these days of volatile public moods. How realistic are the long-range objectives? Are you diversifying as planned? Do spiraling labor costs necessitate change? It's not enough to have well-manicured projections. What are the abstract values inherent in this growth? If you achieve your goals, what do you see emerging as the dominant personality traits of the company? Are you happy with these?

2. *What is your present image?* Elementary? Of course. You can't change, improve or otherwise alter an unknown quality. You may be resourceful and objective enough to do this research yourself, but unless your company is strictly a local operation, professional assistance should be employed. Chances are you'll get some shocks. You can talk all you want to about being a good corporate citizen but you may be as surprised as Republic Aviation was when it learned that its neighbors really had no idea of the company's

78

community involvement. Horn & Hardart considered its reputation for good food at reasonable prices unimpeachable. It was, but it was largely the older people who thought so, research indicated. The younger ones—under 45—preferred restaurants with more atmosphere. Union Carbide assumed that at least the business and financial community knew of its activities but, again, research showed that, despite its size and impact on Wall Street, many analysts simply had no idea of Carbide's over-all size, its diversity, did not know most of its activities and, significantly, did not regard it as an especially forward company.

Ten years ago public relations of AT&T reviewed all current research conducted by the company and its Bell System to determine what over-all image the public had of the telephone business. The mountain of data was impressive but too fragmented to give a true profile. A special Image Study was instituted to get fuller insights. Specifically, it was designed to (a) determine the extent to which various beliefs are held by customers (these beliefs add up to the company's image); (b) to evaluate, insofar as possible, the relative importance of these beliefs, and (c) to determine whether image (or attitude) is related to behavior. Ten basic image areas were identified and the study designed around them. Opinion Research conducted personal interviews with over 1,800 customers. Kenneth P. Wood, assistant vice president of AT&T, summarized the results of the study. In this all-encompassing hypothetical answer the image areas are in italics.

"I'm most impressed by the over-all *quality of your service*. I'm less impressed with your *flexibility in dealing with customers* who have individual problems. I like what I know about your *research*, your management and your *concern for the public interest*. Your *employees* seem to be *well treated* but I can't say too much for the *initiative* they show. I know very little about your *participation in the community* and less about your *local operation*. And, I have real problems with the cost of your service!"

79

Although the customers didn't say so directly, analysis proved that image did affect behavior and that customers with the least favorable image of the telephone company were more likely to complain, and used the phone services least. They also found out a great deal about how the customer viewed the telephone company's size. The results of the study have been used extensively in planning and formulating public relations activities.

A new service, called the Gallup Public Relations Index which will measure corporate public images was announced early this year by Dr. George Gallup, head of the Princeton-based research organization. The service will provide corporations with a continuous, national attitude study of their corporate profiles. The basic profile costs $5,000 and will take 60 days to complete. Twenty-five major industrial firms, all ranking within the top 100 in the nation, signed up initially.

The national corporate image will be broken down into all meaningful classifications. These will include analysis by population, sex, income brackets, political and religious affiliations, ethnic groups, regions and other demographics.

In addition to the general public study, "special publics" or specific areas of interest may be evaluated as well. Included would be a College Study, a Teen-age Study, a Businessmen's Attitude Study, Financial Community Analysis and an Affluent Study (those with incomes over $10,000 a year).

3. *Why do you want to change your image?* * *What*

---

* Five years ago Chemical Company C was unknown to almost half of its public. Its consumer brands, however, were almost universally known, but not conspicuously linked to the corporate name in the company's marketing effort. *The problem: "How can we get greater public familiarity with the corporate name?"* Decision: A comprehensive research and attitude survey was conducted in 1961. It demonstrated that linking consumer brands with the corporate name enhanced the company's over-all reputation. Accordingly, the company made a deliberate effort to identify the corporate name with its consumer brands in all communications (i.e., public relations, advertising, packaging and sales promotion). As a result, Chemical

one do you want to project? Any company that worries about its image in the first place generally wishes to be regarded as the most virtuous of all companies. To the customer it makes the best products; to the stockholder it is an astute money manager; to employees, a benevolent boss; to its neighbors, the town's leading citizen and so on, right down the list of Christian endeavor. Unfortunately, these goals are the same as those of almost every other company. And that's the rub. Saying "me too" will certainly not set your company apart, so try and be a bit more specific, perhaps more candid, about your own goals.

Recognize that a company can't be all things to all its publics. It's as different from the next company as individuals differ. Build on this, don't try to gloss it over into a bland facelessness. And as you wrestle with the riddle of just what sort of personality you'd like to see the company reflect, you'll give your corporate philosophies a good screening. This airing may firm up some that were otherwise buried. The net effect is that you'll discover what is unique about your company. From these you'll determine what is most important and, ultimately, you'll be setting the foundation for corporate goals in the public relations context. The public relations adviser should see in this entire exercise an opportunity, as well as a responsibility, to serve as the catalytic force keeping the study under way and on target until a consensus is reached.

4. *What must be done to freshen up the company's image—and where?* At this point we assume that if any internal changes were called for—a rejuvenation of the product line, a re-structuring within to make the company

Company C gained a greater share of the public mind in a relatively short span of time. In 1961, 55% of the public had heard of the company by its corporate name. Two years after the intensive effort to link products and corporate name, 65% had heard of the company. The latest survey, taken a year ago, indicated that 82% now can identify the company. (A Case Study from the files of Opinion Research Corp.)

more efficient, alert—they've been taken in hand. The job now is to begin surgery on the old image and communicate these changes. It is not purely a question of gearing for accelerated advertising or publicity campaigning. If it's been a drastic face-lifting, all other elements of the company's dress may have to be changed—the trademark, the corporate colors, its letterheads, packaging and everything else that represents it. There is no best way to open the attack. Obviously it should be diversified but it'll be no more effective than the weakest link in the communicating chain. Strong leadership is needed. The public relations and advertising executives can work as co-directors on this if they have rapprochement; your public relations man is elected. He'd better be up to the task. A cardinal rule to be observed is not to forget the "folks at home." Difficult as it is to convince outsiders that the company's made this change for the better, it is even more of an assignment to convince the employees this is so. They have, no doubt, more reason to be skeptical. But convince them you must or the whole rebuilding program will be built on a house of sand.

There are many pitfalls to negotiate in this process of improving the corporate image. For one thing, guard against too much optimism and too much ambition. No matter what the financial, physical and creative resources put on the job, the building of or changing of a company's image cannot be accomplished overnight. Nor within a year. Perhaps within two or three, at the outside. Anyone who tries to sell you an "instant package" is a charlatan. As a matter-of-fact, over-emphasis on near-term (one year) results could lead to the type of frenetic hawking of the company that leaves the company in a state of schizophrenia and the public more disenchanted than before. Excessive pressure to win the public's total affection immediately, without regard to what this all-out drive may have on long term objectives, is both unrealistic and dangerous. Hard-selling doesn't go over in this league. Personal beliefs and opinions, especially among adults, are the toughest of human fabric, and they are changed only with great difficulty. Yet, we know changes do occur; we see evidence of this every day; but consider how reluctantly you change your own views, and you'll get some feeling for the evolutionary process that's involved here.

Second, it cannot be achieved by sleight-of-hand, by gimmicks, or far-out advertising that leans heavily on just being different, and it can't be achieved solely by repackaging the company with new trademarks, color schemes and corporate window dressing.

Third, the cure is not effected simply by endorsing the process of inquiry, analysis and programming. The plan of action derived from such study is not the solution. It represents the means for communicating these changes—a way of identifying the company in a new light. But whether or not the corporate image is successfully changed depends, in the final vote, upon daily company-wide effort to sustain this new attitude. This is the bedrock of a new reputation. We've seen many a new campaign take off grandly in the past, only to lose steam and have all the bright new signs suddenly begin to look a little rusty again because there's been no back-up at home.

The final point and one which applies to the entire spectrum of public relations, not alone to the image-building process: The company is regularly addressing itself to many different publics, each of which is looking at the company differently. True, many of these publics overlap, but they all see the company's image singularly, because their own viewpoints, expectations and motivations vary and give them contrasting perspectives of the company.

All of which reinforces the validity of the total communications concept, with flexible coordination and realistic programming, with the public relations director at or near the helm.

CHAPTER SEVEN

Five Fundamental
Public Relations Targets

You've probably concluded that public relations people resist neat classification, ranging freely from troubleshooter to corporate philosopher, from publicist to company ombudsman. And you are right.

The anointing of a new public relations fellow requires no more preparation than it takes to be a self-styled poet. (However, this rather loose, informal structure is changing; altering its policy of laissez-faire, the Public Relations Society of America in 1965 inaugurated an accreditation program involving a six-hour written examination and a one and one-half hour personal interview by a panel of three examiners who probed applicants' public relations knowledge, techniques and philosophy. Currently some 1,218 members are accredited, and in January, 1969, accreditation will be a prerequisite for active membership.)

Faced with the wide swing in skills and capabilities, management's demands of its public relations department are often beyond the department's ability to supply; in as many other instances, management gears back its expectations to what it deems to be the limit of the capabilities on hand. In either instance this wastes time and money, creates disillusionment and bitterness on the part of management, and darkens its attitude toward public relations. The difficulty any book or guide on the subject faces is to negotiate through this mine field of exposed nerves, while leaving a clear-cut path to follow for satisfaction.

Assume with us, therefore, that your public relations adviser, if he's worthy of this name, will demonstrate some commitment to five fundamental public relations targets. They are: Product publicity (or sales support), the financial community, employees, the community, and a mix of the legislative and economic forces represented in government and labor relations.

You should want to know what level of involvement and degree of responsibility fall to public relations in the average case. Obviously, a well-endowed public relations department has the flexibility and resources to absorb almost all but the crucial policy-setting functions; and even there it should, in many cases, influence.

But what of the more typical, and modest, operations? What guidelines are there to apply as standards? In more than 20 years of applied public relations practice—in a variety of assignments running the gamut of situations from new product introductions to new company formations, from neighborhood speeches to bitter and violent strike conditions —one can see guidelines emerge. The details may change, but the general characteristics of the situations fall into a pattern of replays. What public relations can and should do, as well as what it cannot do, becomes a body of knowledge in itself.

PRODUCT PUBLICITY AND SALES SUPPORT

If there's a moment of truth for the public relations practitioner, it comes when the subject of product publicity is broached. Success in this area comes only to those who can satisfy the insatiable demands made upon creativity, application and perseverance. No wonder many public rela-

85

tions directors are skittish about venturing into this no-man's land. Isolated behind secretaries and organizational charts, they too eagerly agree that this is primarily a function of sales promotion and thus no responsibility of theirs—although, of course, important, from a marketing point of view.

Rot! The introduction of a new product provides the public relations man with one of the few opportunities open to him to make a tangible, rather than a merely philosophical, contribution to the situation, one that can help the profit and loss statement. The public relations man who haughtily disdains involvement in this field is in serious danger of isolating himself from the bread-and-butter profit campaigns of the company. Perspective is an elusive thing; without it public relations expertise can take a Frankenstein-turn into dogmatism. There is no better way to keep perspective fresh than engaging in the daily combat of product marketing.

This single activity mobilizes more elements of the company, theoretically in unity, than almost any other corporate project. Management, employees, sales, engineering, advertising, production are all intimately involved. And so, too, are the stockholders; particularly when the product, as in the case of any one of Polaroid's family of "instant-picture" cameras, has broad impact on future earnings and prospects.

The hard-sell aspects of product publicity and the elemental commercialism inherent in it, sometimes seem to management incompatible with the breadth of background, talents, training and intellectual level of the competent public relations director. To employ such a wealth of talent for so prosaic an assignment seems as spendthrifty as using graduate engineers to write house organ copy. Admittedly, this is an assumption not discouraged by many public relations people.

But these are not the facts of corporate life, especially when we orient our analysis to products that are legitimately new, not products that are new only in terms of the packaging or the copywriter's freshly coined adjectives. We're assuming

86

that the product squarely represents some substantial change from existing or conventional competitive products.

It should be clearly understood that while public relations support, editorially, can be diversified and unusually effective for a new product, it cannot be employed with anywhere near the same impact if the product is merely an "improved" one, dressed up in new packaging or given a new additive. Nor, let us confess, can it do much to convince anyone that "A" is better than the other three well known (and carbon copy) analgesics, or that "Y" deodorant soap is more effective and lasts longer any more than it can prove to a justifiably cynical editor's mind that Dandy-Shine floor wax is brighter, harder and deeper coating than the other two brands. Technically, these are not new products; they're generally cosmetic changes or marketing variations and they cannot be passed off as legitimate new creations. This does not deny the ingenuity of the $27 billion packaging industry.

Often packaging innovations are so tricky and ingenious that they're news in themselves. The black-belt pajamas packaged in a simulated wood box that must be opened with a karate chop certainly rates a news nod, and one can visualize a publicist keeping this alive and in the news by staging karate demonstrations and pitting man against boy in box-opening contests, karate style, of course. But, inevitably, the gimmick will wear itself out and all you have to fall back on is another set of pajamas.

But, if you've got a truly better mousetrap, or automobile tire, skillful publicity can and should be marshaled behind its introduction.

For such, the objective is to sell it. Whether it's sold to a fragmented industry group or the public at large, the marketing ingredients are the same. It must be known; it must be needed; it must be appreciated for what it offers; it must represent value, and it must generate confidence (as to function, service, etc.).

Conventional advertising and sales promotion techniques assume a large burden of this communication headache. But publicity, stemming from sound public relations planning, can add a competitive edge not generally recognized. Product publicity, after all, is in reality one of the oldest and one of the most potent arms of public relations. It is the one facet of this still loosely structured skill that is most closely allied to selling.

Publicity does not mean, simply, reams of commercially toned copy that seeks free space for extolling the virtues of the product. If that were all that were required you wouldn't need a trained public relations man; one or two prolific hacks to grind out stories and invoke the law of averages for success would be cheaper.

But that's like saying that waxing a car makes it ride—and sell—better, overlooking the design, engineering and production that made it in the first place. The public relations man is in the unique position to focus not only on the product but on a variety of elements associated with its creation. Public relations can quarterback the product launching, initiating a flood of editorial activities, building from the following nine basic stages:

Unveil the product—not once but literally hundreds of times.

Promote the ad campaign itself behind the product.

Tell the story of the people who've created it—designers, etc.

Tell the story of the people who've used it.

Report on consumer acceptance.

Report on user reactions.

Tell the story of the product's success.

Tell the story of the company whose name it carries.

Report on trends demonstrated by product.

Then the string can be pulled and much of this done over again on the first birthday, the x hundredth production milestone, etc., etc. And it can be done not only in newspapers, magazines, television, radio and billboards, but by words, photos and cartoons.

Another way to put it is that the public relations campaign taps overlooked resources. After all, a product isn't designed, developed or tested by the salesmen; so those who know most about it are invisible and silent, unless and until publicity draws them into the campaign. We're referring to the designer, engineers, etc.

What they say almost always carries unique believability. None of this happens unless it's new, amusing or unusual. Then it creates attention, interest and, we can assume, word-of-mouth, pass-on attention.

Equally important is the role the public relations director can play in combining and coordinating *all* the communication resources of the company in this project. As an alter ego of management he is in the best seat to overcome the parochial problems and personality differences that often crop up in such situations—i.e., sales vs engineering, engineering vs advertising—and effect the necessary cohesion.

EXTRA AND UNIQUE DIMENSIONS
TO THE SELLING JOB

However elemental the publicity support public relations provides for the launching of a new product, more imaginative use of this resource can lengthen considerably the reach of advertising and marketing programs. It does this on three counts: pre-selling, maintaining sex appeal of existing products, and developing a new product's full market potential via the user's suggestions.

Public relations handling of Bulova's unveiling of the Accutron timepiece demonstrates pre-selling at its optimum and is worth observing. Involved were three—not one—press conferences, a nationwide phone campaign, and a massive letter-writing program—all before a line of advertising appeared.

The rationale was this: The product, Accutron, represented a true technological breakthrough. Yet this created its own special problems. To garner the widest possible audience for its introduction necessitated advance activity. But this jeopardized security. Next, there was the editorial problem of developing a clear understanding of what was a highly technical innovation, without oversimplifying. And, finally, there was the difficult problem of perspective: How to put this breakthrough into its proper light so that Bulova did not simultaneously and automatically imply obsolescence of all of its conventionally made watches. The plan was to conduct an extensive pre-launching educational campaign, organized so as to minimize possibility of leaks.

Working back from media with the longest lead times— the shopping column editors of the monthly home, service and men's publications—three separate and individually tailored (editorially) press briefings were staged. The first was in July, three months prior to "D-Day." It was for the shopping column editors. It was followed in September by an engineering-oriented briefing for technical publications and, finally, in October, the national premiere before 200 members of the general press, in New York and 13 cities via closed-circuit television. The first session was hosted by company marketing people, the second by its technical experts and the third by the top management group. Secrecy was emphasized at the first two, and there were no violations.

Immediately on the heels of the major press unveilings, which resulted in nationwide publicity in major daily newspapers, on radio and TV, in magazines and in columns, the personal letters mentioned in an earlier chapter went from chairman of the board Gen. Omar N. Bradley and president Harry B. Henshel to 5,000 business, scientific and industry officials.

Five Fundamental Public Relations Targets

The letters reported the "breakthrough" and were calculated to stir word-of-mouth notice. Following the premiere, and one week prior to the first advertising of any kind, public relations personally contacted media in the 32 market areas scheduled for advertising, pointing out in localized stories the upcoming ad schedule and the dates of local store unveilings. Color and background feature material was supplied. Additionally, key cities not covered by the telecast were contacted by phone and followed up with a variety of localized stories, features and photographs. In all, 272 editors in 62 cities were personally reached. Then, on December 6, the first advertising broke, nearly six months after the comprehensive pre-selling campaign was launched.

The marketer faces a more difficult problem when the product has existed for some time. How do you maintain sex appeal in a product that's been around for years and years? How do you keep it looking young, glamorous and appealing to the consumer? Advertising and packaging help, of course, but, still, the problem often winds up in the public relations in-basket. An example is the 23-year effort of the Tile Council of America, a marketing, research and public relations arm representing the producers of American-made ceramic tile. Formed in 1945, following a steady downhill sales trend for tile from its pre-war peak of 1926, it had a fundamental objective: To make a product hundreds of years old as appealing as a material fresh out of a test tube. Al McMillan, former executive vice president of Carl Byoir and chief architect of the Tile Council's strategy, and account executive for the first 15 years, recalls the early days. "Let's face it, by itself tile is not newsworthy. So we tried to associate it with cleanliness, sanitation, style and design."

The underpinning of the program was the creation of a research center devoted to discovering new ways to improve tile installations, to keep specifications updated and to devise new uses and design ideas. A nationwide educational campaign pushed the concept of multiple bathrooms in the home

91

(in 1945 the national average was one per home) and expanded the uses of tile by introducing tile design and layouts for kitchens, foyers, patios, playrooms, laundry areas, etc.

The council waged war on foreign imports, taking its case before Congress and the public, and it created a close relationship with builders and architects, entered home shows, sponsored design contests, instituted an architectural scholarship program and launched a national advertising campaign.

The results have been dramatic. Use of ceramic tile zoomed upwards, achieving at one point a 1,100 per cent increase in use, finally leveling off at a rate 10 times greater than its 1945 level.

There's little debate that public relations techniques can stir interest in a new product. Not often, however, is it realized that the publicity generated may accomplish something more strategic than helping sell the product. It may uncover new ways and means for selling the product. Markets are not always known for new products, especially those products that are fully abreast of the state of the art in their field. Many times the full potential of the product itself is more a matter of guess than real knowledge.

Publicity can be effective in identifying the markets or in finding new ones. A case in point is a development that took place a few years ago at Honeywell. The company's research scientists invented an ultra-violet tube that could detect flame, smoke and odor simultaneously. They knew it would be valuable in improving flame safeguard equipment, and it was. But there was a general feeling among the engineers and marketing people that it had potential for many other applications.

An extensive publicity job to report this new development was set off by public relations. It emphasized the trade and technical publications and periodicals, guessing that the native curiosity of engineers and production people would be whetted. They were right; 1600 inquiries resulted. Screening these helped the marketing people compile a list of 50 possible applications they had not previously considered. Some of these have since been successfully developed. It is doubtful that advertising could have generated the same response; perhaps it could have, but it certainly would have been more costly.

HAPPINESS IS TEAMWORK

Teaming up with the sales department can be one of the most satisfying experiences of a public relations man's life—or his most frustrating. Sales is usually the one division of the company that is as committed to change, that is as venturesome and as restless as public relations. Because its bread and butter hinges, as does public relations, on the moods and attitudes of people, it shares common interests and enjoys uncommon rapport with public relations. Nevertheless, there are sales managers with a one-dimensional or limited view of public relations who disrupt the harmony and the effectiveness of this relationship by short-changing it. Public relations, to them, is a long word for publicity, which in turn is a euphemism for free advertising. Their interest begins and ends in newspaper and magazine clippings of hard-sell publicity. Their need is immediate; tomorrow is a space-age term as distant as a budget five years away. Their self-interest is understandable; the pressures for success now, not later, are indeed real. What they fail to remember, however, in their dedicated preoccupation with immediate sales is the intricate relationship between corporate image and attitude toward a product.

To get customers committed to a brand *before* they buy can be done only by pre-selling the company as well as the product. Public relations is a job beyond the scope of the advertising and promotional efforts that support each new product. It is, in fact, the principal objective of corporate

93

or institutional advertising which, as was pointed out in an earlier chapter, is generally a function of public relations, too.

This does not mean that the public relations man, for his part, can take refuge in the long-range munificence of his services to the sales manager (and the company). He cannot, and should not, seek to escape the exacting task of producing product publicity. It's as much a part of his responsibility as the annual report, a community meeting, an employee activity or a reporter's interview with the president. There is no justification for the public relations director's defaulting on this commitment. It may seem trivial in his mind in comparison to more weighty matters awaiting his consideration, but if he's to be involved heart, nerve and muscle in the company, he'll recognize that economic priority prevails. If he has any creative ego, he should respond like a fire horse to the challenge.

A public relations man who's alive and alert will find his own challenge. What problem is older, for example, than that of tying the employee to the selling effort? You'd think that employees would go out of their way to buy their company's products; but, of course, they don't, for some inexplicable reason. Goodyear's public relations department took on this problem as a self-assigned job. They developed a special "Buy Goodyear-Sell Goodyear" program and featured it in the 26 employee newspapers they produce. The newspapers promoted the idea of making all employees members of the sales team by persuading them to get friends, relatives and neighbors to buy Goodyear products. The employees furnished special blanks which were turned in by the purchasers, thereby making the employee eligible for a drawing for free trips to New York, New Orleans, Los Angeles or Las Vegas. Commercial? Of course, but it generated over $500,000 in sales. Among the residual benefits noted was new awareness by employees of the fact that they, too, should buy their own company's products.

Maybe the weight of other matters will keep him from

direct contact on the firing line, but nevertheless he'll employ his insight and his talents to the planning. He knows that selling a product—any product—these days is an immensely complicated operation. Competition is so keen that it is difficult for any company to get and to maintain any distinct advantage over its opposition in terms of such marketing factors as price, distribution, or point-of-sale promotion. No doubt this is one reason why 5,400 out of every 6,000 new supermarket products fail. This means that only one out of 10 makes it.

He knows, too, that commanding even a little of the attention of the target market is a formidable job, because people, in self-defense against the din of some 2,000 messages aimed at them from every quarter daily, tend to tune out all but a fraction. Whether the market is a tightly defined group like doctors, dentists or electronic engineers, or a more expansive one like homeowners or the public at large, he knows he's dealing with a highly unpredictable animal. We've taken the consumer apart, corpuscle by nerve; we've probed his or her psyche, analyzed his alter ego, given each color tests, tachistoscopic tests; exposed him to motivation studies and depth interviews; we've isolated and analyzed his and her living habits, personal habits, secret dreams and wildest aspirations. We can even locate, stratify and quantify present and potential customers. But we still cannot positively predict what they will buy, or how or how much they will buy.

To make maximum impact, obviously the company's story must be told in those places where people form their impressions. How do people get their impressions? One clue is how they spend their time. According to an opinion research analysis,* people in their free time:

watch television	76%
read daily newspapers	70%
listen to radio	63%

* 6,307 interviews—probability sample of U.S. Adult Public.

95

visit or entertain friends or relatives	55%
listen to music	53%
work in the yard or garden	49%
read magazines like *Life, Look, Post,* etc.	42%
watch sports events	39%
read books	36%
read weekly news magazines	26%
travel	31%
go to the movies	23%
participate in sports	22%
pursue hobbies like woodworking, photography, etc.	20%
read business or professional journals	13%
attend plays, opera or ballet	8%

The magnitude of the job of effectively reaching even a sizeable minority emphasizes the practical necessities of combining all communication skills in any marketing program. Coordination is, of course, synonymous with cooperation. One skill has no priority over the other, any more than one wheel outranks another on a bicycle. Because of the multiplicity of publics involved and the necessity of drawing upon corporate resources beyond the normal scope of company marketing forces launching the new product, it falls to public relations' lot to play *a* principal if not *the* principal role. If the "épaulets problem" becomes too severe, this may have to be ordained by executive fiat; no divisive ego problems should be permitted to neutralize this double-pronged effort.

To reiterate, public relations in the product selling situation adds the extra dimension through five major functions.

It helps arouse the prospects' interests—makes them aware of the product, and conditions them for hard-hitting advertising.

It builds depth in the introductory program by its ability to take the story to areas beyond the scope of most advertising schedules—local radio/TV, local papers/house organs/media in 50 states/abroad, etc.

It backs up the salesmen by pre-selling the product. Salesmen can use this news attention as conversation openers, follow-up reminders, or affidavits of interest (or use) and potential sales.

It improves acceptance of a new product by bringing the rest of the company into the act—engineers, designers, etc.—and often stimulates follow-on development activity.

It generates cross-pollination—creates ideas, facts, etc., that in turn might, themselves, form an ad campaign.

FINANCIAL RELATIONS

Management of any publicly owned enterprise that today doesn't recognize and accept the need for maintaining good relationships with its stockholders and the investor and financial community is as rare as a non-union company. Never before have U.S. corporations had to communicate with so vast and varied an audience as they face today. More than 24 million Americans own some part of the 2,300 companies whose stocks are either listed on the stock exchanges or traded over-the-counter. This is a three-fold increase since 1956, and the crest has not been reached, as there has been an 18 per cent increase annually, and there is no indication that it is ending.

Who are these people who want to know more about business? Foremost, of course, is the average stockholder who owns stock in from two to four companies. As is often mentioned, the distaffers own 51 per cent of the outstanding public issues.

One of the most complete investor profiles compiled recently came out of a nationwide poll, in 1968, of 2,200 investors by Paine, Webber, Jackson & Curtis. The strategic value of financial communication is underscored by statistics demonstrating the volatile character of investors. Slightly less than half of the nation's investors made six trades or less in 1967. Some 37 per cent bought or sold stocks between 7 and 24 times. Just 15 per cent made as many as two trades a month. Overall, the typical active investor (someone who buys and sells stock at least 25 times a year) has the following characteristics:

He is 48 years old. (This is about the same as the average age of all shareowners, as reported in the NYSE 1965 Census of Shareowners.)

He is a college graduate. (In the total shareowning population, only about 1 out of 3 are college graduates.)

He has an annual income of $22,000. (In 1965, the NYSE reported the average shareowner income was $9,500.)

Has been investing for at least 10 years.

He owns stock worth $72,000.

Sixty-one per cent of his assets are in stock.

All investors are, of course, consumers; many are business executives, government officials, professional men and women; a large proportion are employees of the company, and a significant number are members of the professional financial community itself, the pipeline through which the company receives its capital. Those who are brokers and analysts for banks, insurance and investment companies, stock-brokerage houses, mutual trust and pension funds, and other financial institutions have a keen appetite for corporate information to help them determine how and where they will add to their large portfolios, and how they will advise their customers on investments.

For years many corporate financial men have encouraged a certain occultism in dealing with the financial community. They've encouraged the belief that the balance sheet and other forms of sophisticated arithmetic pertinent to financial analysis are beyond the translating ability of the public relations man, untutored in the economics of Wall Street.

Some still persist in this moss-grown view; more, however, have recognized that the complexity of the communications problem places much of this burden squarely upon the shoulders of the public relations man.

Management, by and large, realizes that people do not compartmentalize their minds. What they learn as consumers or employees also influences their actions as investors. But this is not an open invitation for public relations, for in this area is still another instance where the statesmanship and diplomatic skill of the public relations man will again be tested. He must establish a harmonious working arrangement with the financial experts of the company. Much of what he will suggest to improve communications may sound heretical to conservative, tradition-bound financial executives. However frustrating this may be, he must accept it as a fact of life and proceed tactfully. He's to start an evolution; not a revolution.

Close study will probably show that the company's financial officers have done a good rudimentary job in communication; that they are in close touch with several key analysts; that they are straightforward and candid with the press. What's missing principally in their operation is dimension—the breadth and scope to give it the impact it fails to generate in the busy marketplace. Some of the intangibles may also be missing, factors many analysts now consider as vital as the conventional data.

For the professional analyst, beyond the price-and-yield relationships, the price-earnings ratio and other irrefutable statistics, there are important intangibles to consider in evaluating the worth of a company. What people think of a company, its management, its philosophies, its attitudes, are intangible but pivotal considerations.

Sidney B. Lurie, research partner for Josephthal & Company, is particularly outspoken on this point. In writing about a company, he is as much motivated by intuition and "feel" as he is by any of the conventional measures. He believes the concept is more important than statistics, per se, and he is personally triggered by what he describes as the "aura of success" about a company, a feeling that develops from innumerable sources—things he's seen, read or heard, and has subsequently checked out.

While less emphatic about it, Robert Stovall, vice president of Nuveen Corporation and for several years research chief of a major wire house, said his firm's staff gives considerable weight to opinions expressed about a company in responsible media, perhaps even more than to opinions or conclusions reported by the financial services. Such services, he says, are valuable for the statistics, but often more reliable impressions of management and a company's capability can be gleaned from such sources as *Business Week, Forbes, Barron's* and other principal financial media. E. F. Hutton's research library, for example, subscribes to some 200 periodicals, including newspapers, and scans them daily, transmitting appropriate news items via its own morning wire service to its 40 branch offices.

It is obvious that the analysts' research must today go far beyond such purely financial matters as dividend records, stock splits and merger possibilities, beyond sales and earnings records and price earnings ratio. They must study the company's products, physical facilities, management and marketing strategy, labor relations and its corporate "image." Often it is relevant to assess the future of an entire industry, bringing into consideration such factors as technological advance, national economic and social policies, and world affairs.

THE "OUTSIDE" SPECIALISTS

Thus, the revolution in financial communication, plus the galloping merger movement (a 37 per cent increase to 2,384), has given impetus to a new breed of financial communicator, the specialized financial relations firm, the

100

proxy solicitation experts and the investor relations professionals. Manufacturing and mining companies alone in one year recorded 279 mergers in the first quarter, 372 in the second, 377 in the third and 468 in the fourth.

While many of these firms offer, on paper, a broad range of communication services, their expertise focuses on the merger action: defending against a tendered offer or initiating one. They are expert at mobilizing a company's resources to defend or to attack. With the proliferation of conglomerate companies there's been no shortage of work for these specialists.

But usually they've neither the organization, the time nor even the temperament to conduct the day-in-day-out, bread-and-butter communication with the financial and investment community essential to a company's long-term health and growth. In this it is the consistency as well as the quality and quantity of the information communicated that spells the difference.

Today we're in an era of constant financial communication. Companies are vying with one another for the attention and approbation of stockholders, investors and the entire financial community with torrents of interesting, provocative information. A great many companies lose out in this severe competition for analysts' time for sheer lack of visibility; many a good performance record gets only a fraction of the notice and understanding it merits, simply because analysts just do not have the time to dig into every company as deeply as they might.

Keith Funston, former New York Stock Exchange president, said the question is no longer whether or not the public should be informed about significant corporate developments but how best this can be accomplished; not whether the corporate community has definite responsibilities to the public, but how these can best be fulfilled.

The Exchange offers a guide to companies that profiles 200 examples of corporate communications in 22 major categories. They range from the mandated communications, annual and interim and quarterly reports to such relatively new techniques as post-meeting reports, economic education booklets, special financial fact books with detailed statistical data for analysts, and films and speeches.

The magnitude of the job of broadening financial communication precludes its remaining bottled up within the financial department of a company. The open-handed, free-wheeling creativeness and objectivity of the public relations man is better suited to this assignment. For his own part he must deepen his own knowledge of the business and financial aspects of the company, so that in translating the language of business into the language of the layman he maintains the basic integrity of the facts.

It is the diversity of the financial relations objectives of most companies that underscores why this communications job has grown far beyond the capabilities of the financial department. Reporting on how the company met its fiduciary responsibilities is only the beginning, the tip of the iceberg; hidden from sight are a host of other considerations requisite to putting a company in better focus with the business and financial community. Companies, of course, differ as to specific objectives but, in general, they fit into the ten following communications goals:

To report on management's stewardship of the company.

To strengthen its reputation with present stockholders.

To attract new stockholders.

To broaden knowledge of the company, as fundamental to helping set a fair market price for its stock.

To build good relations with regulatory agencies and tax authorities.

To get stockholders' support of management, primarily reflected in disposition of their proxies.

To develop new sources of capital.

To encourage stockholders to purchase the company's products.

102

To broaden ownership of the company.

To make friends among institutional stockholders and the financial community.

To accomplish these objectives is as much a matter of attitude and philosophy as it is programming and action. The approach to it cannot be how little can you get by with telling analysts, but how much further can you go in informing them without seriously impinging on the operations of the company, competitively or otherwise.

For example, it is not enough to respond to analyst inquiries, no matter how enthusiastically. A company has to take the initiative to bring its story to the financial community if analysts are to have all the information necessary for an accurate appraisal. This is a subtle point, lost on some financial people. Consider a hypothetical example that typifies a prevalent attitude. For years ABC company has established and maintained valuable and close relationships with key elements of the financial community. The company has been candid and responsive to inquiries from both analysts and financial news writers and, as a result, there's been generated a fair amount of visibility. All in all, it's been a respectable effort.

But is it enough today? Closer analysis will usually show that the job, however commendable, still falls short on two counts by today's new and tougher communications ground rules.

One, since the initiative for the information exchange comes almost exclusively from without, this tends to create a reasonably informed cluster of analysts, but it is a small and limited group, possibly excluding more dynamic financial areas (i.e., mutual funds, investment trusts, etc.) that could be effectively responsive to the company's story. Lacking any significant feedback from the company, their reports may leave something to be desired in terms of balance and accuracy (updating's a headache), and may even overlook small but pertinent details. Further, there is the distinct probability that the security analysts' characterization has settled into a sterile format that can little excite or stimulate a new or broader interest in the company. It is difficult enough for analysts to keep abreast of the economic changes within a company; to expect them to pick up the tenuous changes in its personality, or the nuances of its mood or direction is not in the cards. Chances are that their portrayal of the company is bland, lacking any substantive feeling for its management versatility or depth, for its R&D, or its technological know-how. In short, there's probably nothing to lift the company out of the crowd, to distinguish it, to give it some flavor of a company on the move or of one highly competitive and creative (assuming, of course, that it is all that). There are obvious exceptions to this, but the in-depth coverage for such glamour stocks as Xerox, IBM, and Control Data are really the exceptions that prove the rule. They're evidence of the perceptive reporting that can be done if the analysts are sufficiently motivated. For many of the blue chips and hundreds of companies on the periphery, this motivation has to be encouraged and nurtured like the fragile flower it is. (This does not imply that the success stories of Xerox and the others were products of propaganda; these companies created attention primarily because they were *creating* their own futures, not just planning or talking about it. The analysts brought these stories out like news reported, and gave them perspective.)

This brings us to the second shortcoming in the competition for attention. If a company waits until it is asked to be heard, its voice will be weak and feeble against the trumpeting of all its competitors. The average analyst's work day schedule ties him up with administrative duties and with monitoring as many as 250 stocks in five to six industries, 30 to 50 of which he watches closely, and perhaps five that he studies intimately and intently. This leaves about two per cent of his time to look into new issues or to investigate other companies. Much of this analysis is facilitated by the industrial classifications, i.e., electronics, building stocks, etc. But some companies, including many of the conglomerates, just don't fit neatly into a category. They may not be overlooked, but it may take a long time to work their way out of the pending file. Considering the 2,300 listed stocks plus the large number of over-the-counter issues, the chances for him to pick your company are about as good as your winning a lottery—*unless* something directs his attention to your company, again, something he's seen, read or heard about. To get such conversation going about your company simply means that you cannot wait for financial news to happen; it must be created. Not only must this material be generated in volume but its distribution to media must be diversified to cater to the reading and information-gathering habits of members of the financial community. Repetition is the common denominator of this opinion-building action.

While the specific content of the material to form the basis of this dialogue will vary from company to company, generally speaking the following are considered requisites for a sophisticated evaluation of a company's investment character:

It should identify the company's ability to be competitive in diversified markets.

Or highlight the company's market power (penetration) or market leadership.

Or create awareness of its research and technological capabilities.

Or give insight into its future plans and programs.

Or identify and underscore its management depth and capability.

Or record its determination to be an efficient and cost-conscious producer.

These points, individually and collectively, encapsulate a host of intangibles that analysts, brokers and financial writers are responsive to in forming opinions about a company. Perhaps they seem too perfect, too pat. They are, after all, superlatives every company aspires to and generally lays claim to. The public relations man's job is to substantiate his company's claim to any or all of these, and communicate in a manner that is convincing to objective and often cynical outsiders.

A former president of the Investment Analysts Society of Chicago (the first of its kind in the country), George H. Norton, Jr., vice president of the Continental Illinois National Bank and Trust Company, Chicago, says that one of the main jobs—and perhaps the trickiest—of the financial analyst is to get a fix on the corporate or management philosophy. Facts and figures are essentially a matter of history. The future growth, however, hinges upon a reading of management's aims and objectives and the potential ability of management to reach its goals.

Norton suggests full candor; let management identify some of its problems and then explain what it's doing to overcome or solve them. He believes that the process of identifying problems and solving them is the most telling exposition of management's capability it is possible to demonstrate. Unfortunately, but understandably, management, unless it has the solutions well in hand, will rarely be moved to explain how it is temporarily stumped by this or that problem. But Norton's point is well taken because it touches the nerve of this communications problem: analysts don't want warmed-over statistics served up that they can get from Moody's, Standard and Poor's or the company's latest report. They are, however, interested in any meaningful data that will enable them to make better-informed judgments.

FACE-TO-FACE CONTACT

Communication, in the context of better financial relations, involves much more than the printed word. Here, as in innumerable other areas involving attitude change, there is no substitute for personal contact. It is through face-to-face contact that analysts not only sound out management on its basic operating policies but also appraise its frankness and the confidence with which it answers questions, and obtain an intuitive feel for the intangibles mentioned earlier that contribute to a company's personality and reputation.

These contacts may be one-on-one situations at the company headquarters, where the analyst has called, or in small eight-to-ten person meetings, or the major address before one of the Financial Society meetings. Even though written communication is not essential here, the public relations man should be intimately involved, because more communications mistakes have been made in this area than in the others. Perhaps it is because the company's financial experts strongly feel that here, at least, is one operation in which they will call the tune; after all, they speak the analyst's language and they know what he wants to hear and certainly it's not the ghost-written, public relations oriented "sell." So company financial vice president after vice president traipses down to a financial analyst luncheon meeting and proceeds to bore his so-called brethren to tears. In New York, such company presentations meandered so far off target that the New York Society of Security Analysts seriously considered offering to write, or help the company prepare, its own presentation. Again, this is not a blanket criticism of all corporate speeches, nor a blackball for all financial vice presidents and treasurers. However, speeches that are done well professionally utilize, you can be sure, the resources of their public relations people. But there are still enough reluctant financial dragons who will brook no interference, and will accept little outside (of their department) counsel on the organization of their companies' presentations to analysts, to keep the problem an active one.

It is paradoxical that with the mushrooming of financial communications there are still such glaring soft spots in the most critical of all areas of communication, the face-to-face

107

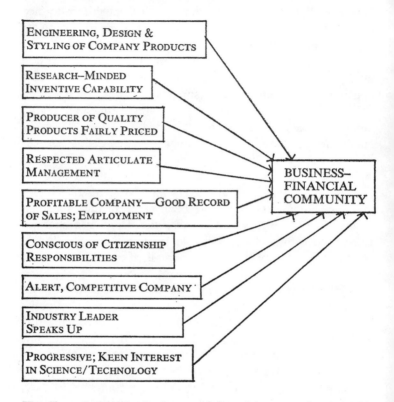

The "image" that the business and financial community has of a company is a product of the sum total of a number of considerations, nine of which are shown here. The criteria differ, of course, from company to company, but what does not differ is that the analyst's impression of a company is built on any number of smaller, perhaps more subtle, impressions.

encounters. Twelve years ago, the then president of the Investment Analysts Society of Chicago laid down some ground rules for building a presentation to analysts. Time—and evolution—has not erased the need for such guidelines, so George Norton felt obliged to cite them again when he was president of the group in 1966—and they're no less timely today. You might call them the rules of common sense because the logic behind each is crystal clear. A skilled communicator, i.e., the public relations adviser, would instinctively follow the same guidelines because he recognizes that the key to communication is to give people information that *they want,* not what you want them to have. Here are those guidelines:

DON'TS

It is not necessary to go into a long corporate history.

Most of us are aware of the plant locations of a company. Unless something new and of unusual importance can be brought out, the analysts would be gaining no new knowledge by a mere listing of plant locations.

Industry background is fine, but it is not necessary to take up much time talking about this. Perhaps such data could be included in a brochure that could be left at the table or distributed at the door as the analysts leave the meeting.

Some companies make good use of a fact book. It gives the analysts historical data and makes an excellent addition to the research files. Also, it means that the officers telling the story of a company need not go into detail in their talk.

Many corporate officials feel that it is necessary to do some "flag waving" about the American way of life and the competitive system. Please be assured we investment analysts believe in this competitive system, and such a presentation is not necessary.

A sales pitch without documentation is of little value. However, we would expect a corporate executive to be enthusiastic about his company. But, be sure to document the reasons for this enthusiasm.

It is not necessary to comment in detail about the annual report. We undoubtedly all have copies of this report available and to go into detail is merely a rehash of something we should have done on our own.

While people are extremely important in a company, it is not desirable to spend too much time emphasizing their importance in an organization. In other words, don't dwell on this unless you can isolate some real leadership and discuss how this leadership has been developed. On the other hand, comments about the way in which management identifies potential leadership and nurtures it could be useful. Here again, it's like the sales pitch; a discussion of people in general is of little help. A discussion of people with documentation can be very useful.

DO'S

We do feel that a discussion of sales is necessary. Quarterly sales figures are quite important. Management sometimes says that quarterly figures are of little help, for it is so difficult to set up an appropriate accounting approach to getting good quarterly data. However, we feel, as analysts, that quarterly figures are important for they do denote a trend. If there are unusual activities represented in the sales figures, these could be footnoted or explained. This merely says, therefore, that good accounting and reporting demands footnoting and explanation and this refers to annual reports as well as quarterly reports.

We feel that sales should be defined in more detail, i.e.: Break out sales on a gross basis or a no profit basis. In other words, any subsidiary of a company or any part of a company which accounts for 15 per cent or more of sales and/or profit should be identified and this information made available.

We frequently get the explanation that a detailed breakdown of sales figures would be of comfort and aid to the competition. This might be true. However, as we analysts talk to competitors around the country, we are aware that the competitors already have a very clear picture as to what portion of the market another company may have, and even a very good idea as to the profitability of a given segment of a company's operations. We feel that sales should be "broken down" to represent the type of operations. This is almost a classification by industry, especially in a conglomerate company.

Customer classification is also very useful. We are aware that some companies have a few major customers who account for a large portion of the sales.

Profit margins certainly should be discussed. It is quite necessary to ascertain the trend of profit margins and explain.

Backlogs of business should be noted.

We feel that it is quite necessary to discuss the competitive picture and pricing situation. A discussion of the pricing picture gives us a clue to management's ability to watch the markets and to compete.

We would like to know about new products. We don't expect management to tell us about products that are still in the developmental stage. However, where new products are about to enter the market, we would like a discussion of the potential. Especially, we would like to know how management defined and analyzed the market in deciding to go ahead with the distribution of a given product. All of this really says "tell us about your marketing philosophy." Marketing know-how is very important not alone to the company, but to the analyst, as he tries to get a feel of management's over-all philosophy. Also, the analyst would like to know something about production planning and how closely production is geared to marketing.

We would like information concerning plant expansion and modernization.

We would like to know about capital spending plans.

Capital spending means financing likely will be necessary. Thus, some discussion of financing requirements and the affect on the capitalization of a company is desirable.

111

We would like management to discuss its acquisition and merger philosophy. Again, we are not expecting management to divulge any secrets. It is the basic philosophy of acquisition and merger that we would like to have brought to our attention.

A representative of the long-range planning area of the business should be present. What is the planning for the future? What is being done to improve profit margins? What about product development plans? What is the marketing strategy for the future? What about selection or identification of leadership in the evaluation and training of people?

TIMELY DISCLOSURE

Not since the early days after the Civil War, when the New York Stock Exchange made the controversial proposal that all listed companies make annual financial statements available to their stockholders, has there been such emphasis on company-sponsored financial communication. And, in recent years, the element of time has been introduced. Speed in releasing is of paramount importance. Today, both the Exchange and the Securities & Exchange Commission insist that companies, in addition to the release of conventional earnings, merger and acquisition news, make news of major new products, and discoveries, contract awards, and expansion plans subject to the same "timely" or "immediate release" policy. Of equal importance is the prompt reporting, clearly and fully, of any unfavorable news that may affect the public's appraisal of the value of the company's stock. If the preparation of such material in full promises to unduly delay its release, then a digested announcement should be made, followed with the longer, more detailed statement.

Whether the news is good or bad, restraint, good judgment and advance planning can ordinarily keep things in proper perspective. The most ticklish problems arise when important confidential deliberations are under way. Prudent public relations practice suggests that the market action of the stock be watched closely, as well as any unusual pattern of analyst calls—with the view of issuing a preliminary statement if necessary.

Regardless of the means used to release information—messenger, telephone, teletype, telegraph—it is not considered "public" until it *actually appears* in public print or in or on other public media. As the expert in communication, the public relations man has the duty to use his best judgment to choose among the various communications methods available to him which will best help his company comply with the timely disclosure requirements of the Exchange and the SEC.

There are stringent rules imposing restrictions on the communications a company can engage in at the time it's undertaking a new stock offering and when its stock is in registration. What financial news can be reported during these periods must be delicately handled. It is the public relations adviser's job to be intimate with the latest rulings covering these situations and to work closely with the company's financial department on the day-to-day handling of corporate news. It is not the SEC's intention to invoke a complete news embargo on the company, but the standard it imposes on the legitimacy of such news is severe.

WHERE TO CENTER CONTROL

The investor/financial relations program (they're sometimes lumped into one) gets its basic policy direction from the chief executive officer, the chief financial officer and/or the board of directors.

All of the communications creativity and person-to-person stratagems that might be employed would be a paper-thin façade unless they are supported—indeed, stem from—

113

an enlightened, active investor and financial relations policy base. A distinction should be made between investor relations and financial relations, although it may be drawing a fine line. The former involves, obviously, stockholder and analyst contact; the latter covers these two—from a communications point of view—as well as the strategically important financial news media.

Then, of course, there is the day-to-day financial housekeeping, in which public relations has no business getting involved. From capital requirements and inventory control to new stock offerings, there's a full inventory of fiduciary responsibilities that underpin the overall policy.

And this policy is, as it should be, set by the financial executives of the company. If it's an enlightened, healthy program, communications will be so integral to it that it may appear sometimes that public relations, per se, is in charge. If it is, it shouldn't be; it'd be a case of the tail wagging the dog, but with more disastrous consequences.

Nevertheless, as has been pointed out, the central problem is in the dissemination, judiciously and equitably, of pertinent information that would help stockholder and analyst alike to gain a better perspective on the company. Financial men—lawyers, accountants, comptrollers, et al.—are not by training and avocation the best judges of what is news and how to transmit it effectively. Nor are they necessarily the best equipped to weigh the quality of the existing relationship with either investors or the financial community. They're much too involved to be objective; and even if they could step away from it and try to get an overall view, they've not the right yardsticks by which to measure the performance.

But in collaboration with public relations, much progress can be made. Together they should review the company's philosophy of investor/financial relations. Maybe it needs reassessing, updating. An audit of where the company stands *vis-à-vis* the professional financial community would seem to be in order. Once knowing where the company is, in the eyes of the investment experts, it can determine where it would like to be and what it will take to get there. Internal procedures for handling analysts should be reviewed, external contacts studied. Inevitably, this leads to improvements in communications, both written and verbal. But lest the public relations man be carried away by his brilliance, he should remember that counseling is defined as giving opinion and instruction to direct the conduct of another. It does not guarantee the wisdom to act on that advice nor does it imply that such advice will become policy.

WATCH YOUR LANGUAGE

Factual integrity and policy evaluations are not the only criteria to be applied to communications. Always hovering over the writer's shoulder these days are the watchful eyes of the anti-trusters. They've found fertile pickings in the unguarded statements of corporations. In some cases these have had greater impact in the courts than detailed economic presentations. Unwise and perhaps naïve statements and expressions have often turned out to be the government's missing link in weaving a *prima facie* case against a company, and they've been key evidence leading to a decision against a company.

The trend at the present time seems to place unusual emphasis on the written word—or oral statement—in anti-trust cases. Careless statements relating to market share, reciprocity, or competitive power—to name but three areas of hazardous wordsmanship—are sufficient to provide the burden of proof in many instances.

A classic example is the pivotal weight given to a Procter & Gamble statement which said in part: ". . . taking over the Clorox business . . . could be a way of achieving a

dominant position in the liquid bleach market quickly. . . ."
The Federal Trade Commission successfully blocked this
merger.

John T. Loughlin, one-time assistant general counsel to
the Federal Trade Commission, and now in private practice,
listed ten naughty words of anti-trusters in a provocative
article in the *American Bar Association Journal* (Vol. 54,
March, 1968). He identified the following words as high in
the anti-trusters' search file: guilt complex words, i.e., please
destroy after reading; power words; planning and intent
words, i.e., to take over a market; words delineating markets
or market share, i.e., to get 50 per cent of a market, etc.;
bragging words; overselling words; special offers contrary to
Robinson-Patman; over-competitive words, i.e., to cut prices
to penalize a competitor, or to deprecate a competitor's
capability; words disparaging a competitor, i.e., exploiting, in
writing, his weaknesses; loose words about competitors and
prices; helpfully intended words by friends—these are the
most difficult to guard against. Honest misinterpretations by
investment houses as to "virtual monopoly," "market domina-
tion," and like phrases used to profile a company's activities,
can be legally disastrous.

All of this only serves to emphasize what every public
relations man worth his title has burned into his subconscious:
There is no substitute for judicious choice of language in
releases, annual reports, inter-company memorandums and
other communications to shareholders, notwithstanding pressure of time, project or circumstance—or ignorance or gulli-
bility.

EMPLOYEE RELATIONS

The modern corporation, which is about 100 years old,
has pretty well outlived its public image of the 1920s and

116

'30s—that of a faceless trust or soulless bureaucracy swallowing up humans in a pitiless struggle for power and profit. The vast changes that have taken place and are still evolving in our society have had profound impact on the corporation both sociologically and technologically as a social institution. The corporation is not today what it was in the past, and it will not be in the future what it is today. The new dynamism of the corporation—the revolution taking place in its social structure—has been examined, diagnosed, probed and psychoanalyzed by scholars, sociologists, historians and businessmen, themselves. The Kaiser Corporation, in an extraordinary monograph, *The Corporation as a Creative Environment,* sees the corporation as being in the throes of a massive revolutionary transition from a monolithic bureaucratic hierarchy to an increasingly democratic, free-form team operation. Regardless of how extreme or modified your view, there is no denying that the corporation is reacting sensitively to a fast-changing technology that swirls about it and, also (and this is of deeper concern to the public relations adviser) that it is reacting to the internal pressures brought about by the emergence of a new breed of employee. Today, men and women are, on the whole, better educated, better trained and differently motivated than their parents were; their psychological background makes them more likely to resent authority than to respect and obey it.

The challenge, and need, of dealing effectively with the highly complex social organization of the corporation—of somehow blending and balancing the myriad personalities that inhabit it into a workable, productive team that will forward the ambitions and goals of the corporation—has become a science, not an art. The intuitive judgments of management are no longer equal to the task of establishing and maintaining a healthy relationship between all echelons of the corporate family. It requires highly trained and experienced personnel and industrial relations specialists. They are generally on top

117

of the situation, and the last thing needed is gratuitous advice or Monday morning quarterbacking from the public relations man.

This does not by any means make this area off-limits to the public relations management, but it suggests the need for caution in injecting its expertise. For, while the resident personnel savants may know what applied psychological principles motivate employees to more productive output, it inevitably comes down to putting their knowledge to practical application. There is no short cut to this, and it leans heavily, as it must, on effective communication.

Policy without the program to implement it (communicate) is a dull tool. In the final analysis, what you're dealing with are honest efforts to reach the employees, to change if necessary their attitudes, their habits or their opinions. Increasingly, companies are obliged simply to try to keep employees as fully informed of corporate action as is feasible and, of course, considerably more emphasis is placed these days on generating an accurate feedback of what the employees are thinking. Few companies will deny the priority of the latter, but it is a fact that many of these very same corporations will, in fact, conduct their employee relations communications program in the classic "pipeline" tradition: fill it up at the top and pour it out at the bottom—as though attitude change is simply a question of providing sufficient piping of facts to the personnel. The less they respond, the heavier the dosage. A Grade One sociologist will tell you that it just doesn't work that way. Behavioral change cannot be equated with information. In fact, inundation of information may have the opposite effect; it can force the subject to resist changing his mind even more strongly, as he digs in his heels psychologically against the information onslaught.

Public relations, in the context of the perimeters we've established for it, has the fundamental responsibility to involve itself in any area in which there is a relationship to be established between management and a group of people; and certainly there is no more critical area of people than the employees. Despite this blanket mandate, productive involvement of public relations here must be accomplished through and with the support of personnel management. Whatever the frustrations may be in establishing this relationship, it must be done in straightforward fashion. This is still another instance where the public relations man must show some humility; he is not the panacea for *all* of the company's problems; nor is he by divine right the knighted expert to free-wheel the restructuring of the corporation, even though he does uncover grave public relations faults.

The headaches of dealing with attitude change and communication with employees present riddles enough for most personnel people for them to welcome any constructive aid. They need no reminder, or public relations oriented analysis, to appreciate that the old trusted in-house media standbys—the bulletin board, house organ, plant newspaper, pay envelope stuffer and inter-office memo—are hardly adequate to the integrated communications activity requirements of a modern corporation. Even those techniques have undergone significant changes editorially. Company publications—newspapers, for instance—are becoming less middle-of-the-road or bland. Management finds little economic merit in trying to bend over backwards not to express its opinion. McGraw-Hill, in describing the editorial objective of its weekly newspaper, the *News,* says that while its readers' likes and preferences are important to it, these will not shape editorial policy or content. It says, quite candidly, that it doesn't believe publications are two-way streets any more than loudspeakers are.

A house organ is started to do a job for a company. And the preferences of employees (editorially) cannot be permitted to divert management from presenting the sort of information that the company feels is in the best interest of the organization. The real job, as they see it, is to get employees to like and to read some of the useful and important

119

information that the company wants to communicate. The company paper cannot shape its sentiments to the pleasures of the public. Needless to say, the *News* has an avid audience, and a high degree of credibility; many readership surveys testify to the value of the publication as an industrial communicator.

The *News* is by no means exceptional. Among the more than 4,000 company publications produced, there are literally hundreds that measure up by editorial and journalistic standards to the best of the commercial publications. Some, like DuPont's *Better Living,* are slick, professionally-produced magazines that are as creative and interesting as any of the newsstand variety. Honeywell's *World* was created by and edited for years by one of Minnesota's top newspaper editors who left the Minneapolis *Tribune* to take on the assignment. The *World,* which reports on company activity on three continents, has been a major communicating force linking a company now represented in 25 nations.

This illustration is not intended to position company publications as the most valued technique in employee relations, but to demonstrate how the new sophistication of this one vehicle for communication reasserts the need for greater involvement of the counsel and the technical skills of the public relations specialists. They will augment, not supplant, the corporate talents already charged with the primary responsibility in this area.

The objective of any employee relations program is to establish a basis for understanding, for management and employees to know and respect each other, to understand each other's motives and objectives even if there is disagreement as to content or concept. Every day a corporation makes hundreds of decisions, any one or all of which could ultimately affect the economic future of employees. And every day employees discuss the company, exchange opinions and form attitudes that may ultimately inhibit the corporation's freedom to act or to react to change.

None of this will change as a result of highly-powered internal communications machinery. But a soundly conceived and professionally executed program of idea, opinion and information exchange can at least minimize the misinformation and the misunderstandings, and create a neutral climate for discussion.

Sociologists tell us that people act to satisfy their own needs and desires, not the needs of an organization, except as they are obliged to for economic security. Nevertheless, employees *can* be motivated by emphasis, not on the benefits to the corporation, but by emphasis, for example, on the benefits and satisfaction he or she will gain from this action. This is a rudimentary illustration of the relative importance of what is communicated over how it is transmitted. Public relations can be helpful here, technically in the professional treatment of the communications form, but of even more strategic assistance in the identification of what motives to appeal to in any particular campaign.

It is in this area that most organizations make their most serious mistakes.

Once the decision is reached to open fuller communications with employees, the execution, to the unprofessional communicator, seems cut and dried. The means for reaching employees—the most captive of all audiences—appears uncomplicated and routine. Deceptively so. After all, write them a letter and they'll read it; put a notice on the bulletin board and they'll scan it; publish a newspaper and they'll give it at least a once-over. Stuff a notice in their payroll envelopes and you can be sure they won't throw it away until they've looked at it.

But will they believe any of what they've read? Is it paternalistic? Too self-serving? Or, maybe it's just irrelevant or immaterial to them. Only if you've been involved in the daily combat of gaining people's attention will you fully appreciate the subtle hurdles that must be overcome. Marshall McLuhan to the contrary, the medium is *not* the message, certainly not in employee relations! The old obsolete "pipeline" theory of pouring the information on as the problem grows, simply will not do the job.

There's an apt saying that in much of talking thinking is half murdered. To put it another way, the exchange of views cannot be limited to the outflow from management. What about the information flow from the bottom up? The desire to get through to management is not confined to those in the better-educated echelons; the clerical staff and the factory work force have as strong an urge to get the ear of top management. Often this is difficult, if not impossible. Perhaps there's no system that permits it. Maybe the intermediate supervisory level is reluctant to rock the boat, so it shuts off any such request that might disturb the status quo. Conditions such as these, and they're not uncommon even today, create hostile environments for communication. Employees reflect their frustrations in their approach to corporate information; they're decidedly negative, even cynical, about the information they receive from management.

Personnel management is not without its own resources to cope with these situations. It recognizes, for example, if it's a top-flight staff, that supervisory personnel themselves are often ill-equipped to be an effective communications bridge from management. Well-meaning but inarticulate foremen can unwittingly sabotage the best-laid plans. So, personnel sets up training programs, holds briefing sessions, calls group meetings, stages company affairs, revamps its communications program and, in general, uses its skill and creativity to improve the techniques. But sometimes they, too, are thwarted, either by a lack of direct contact with top management on the policy aspects of the changes they'd like to introduce, or more generally, with the apparent ineffectiveness of their own communications effort. Public relations management can offer new resources to solve the problem. First, the direct bridge to higher management, if necessary. Second, the advisory and technical services to re-orient the

122

communications effort. Working closely with personnel, considerable progress can usually be made and formats established that will not require the daily participation of the public relations staff, although the effectiveness of the program will continue to be of concern to them.

Complicating this communications matter is the rapidly expanding need for management to explain its involvement (or, worse, its inertia) in the urban crises that are pulling industry in deeper and deeper. This is the latest in the long inventory of social responsibilities being laid at the door of the corporation. A great deal hinges, not alone on how forcefully the corporation acts, or even when, but how this is translated and interpreted to the employees. After all, this is the primary audience, simply because it *is* the family. It's an old adage of public relations that *it* begins at home. This may sound like too much of a truism to be fashionable these days, but you cannot escape its simple truth.

Management would naturally like to have some measure of the effectiveness of its communications effort short of discovering, in the turmoil of a strike, that nobody had been listening. While its own apparatus of communication leans heavily on the formal media tools (print and film), the employees are less inclined to write things out. They are more at ease in face-to-face or oral communication.

In taking stock of employees' absorption of the communications output, one should not put too heavy a reliance on formal attitude surveys. The reports of middle management, supervisors, plant and factory personnel are likely to be more objective. Personnel undoubtedly has firm views on how best to get this insight and, with encouragement from public relations, will develop realistic methods for generating the feedback necessary.

The central role public relations plays in employee relations is that of a "devil's advocate," tactfully but firmly initiating a review of the system. It would ask such questions as:

123

Is it operating by rote? Or is it a viable, dynamic operation?

How flexible is it? Is it rigidly structured to unchanging deadlines and budgets?

Is it diversified? Creative? Or just the mechanical media (i.e., bulletin boards, house organs)?

How does it get its policy inputs? Does it get any, other than corporate censorship?

Scanning a six month's supply, how does all of it rate on coverage of corporate appointments, company's financial position, benefits and wages, job security protection, operating problems, news of major corporate activities, news of corporate competitors, work of other plants or divisions?

Going beyond the mechanics of the communications process, public relations, in consultation with personnel, should endeavor to weigh the comprehensiveness of the entire process by seeking the answers to such questions as:

How good is the communication between management and supervisor, or between the salaried employee below the supervisory level?

How often and in what form is the contact made between management and the union officials; between union management and employee management and the same employees?

How frequent is the formal communication between middle management and top management?

What is the proportionate flow of information down from the top to the bulk of employees versus the information flow upwards?

Scoring would be 5 for *ideal;* 4 for *satisfactory;* 3 for *adequate;* 2 for *getting by but needs improving;* 1 for *bad.* Add the totals and divide by the number of answers. Passing grade is 3½, and even that's a signal for some serious reviews and improvements.

There is one final and overriding influence public relations can have on the conduct of employee relations. Through tactful monitoring it can make certain that there is no discrepancy in the discussion of corporate policy points. This is not to imply that personnel would be less than exact about these considerations, but often, in the daily press of activity, variations and nuances creep in that, in total, can alter the fundamental meaning. Further, there is nothing rigid or sacrosanct about policy; it is being changed daily, and the public relations adviser may well be more current.

LABOR RELATIONS

Few areas test the technical skills and judgments of the public relations man as does that of labor relations. While there's no denying his legitimate participation, there are severe limitations placed on his freedom of action. After all, what is essentially involved is people: the relationship of employees with their labor unions, on one hand, and with the company on the other.

For one thing, there are necessarily policy considerations set down by management. Second, there are the lawyers. The legal technicalities that abound in modern collective bargaining contracts have to all intents and purposes put the lawyers in charge. Few lawyers will claim that legal training is appropriate for the delicate job of communicating with employees on labor union matters. Unfortunately, this candor does not generally carry over when the actual work of communicating is attempted. Public relations people must expect and accept, with good grace, the red tape and the frustrating shackles placed on their efforts.

If a reasonably sophisticated job of employee relations is in-being, the specific work of communicating relative to union contracts has a firm foundation upon which to build. Hopefully, therefore, credibility has been established for management's statements.

The functioning of labor relations is a line responsibility

of the plant or divisional management. Most union contracts are all-encompassing, spelling out work procedures around-the-clock and anticipating most contingencies. One of the few remaining areas still open to management prerogative is communication with their employees, although even that is repeatedly being challenged.

When P. R. Mallory & Co. wrote a series of four letters to employees during an organizing drive by the AFL-CIO International Union of Electrical Workers, the National Labor Relations Board ruled that the letters constituted coercion and restraint in violation of the labor laws. NLRB said the letters threatened the workers with adverse economic consequences, including loss of work or jobs, if they designated a union. However, an appeals court later upheld the employer's letters as being free speech, protected under the law. The court said that an employer is free to tell his employees what he reasonably believes will be the likely economic consequence of unionization—those consequences that are outside of his control.

It remains to be seen whether this common-sense decision will further protect freedom of speech for employers, as well as for unions. The case graphically shows the potential pitfalls existing and the complex delicacy involved in what would seem to be a routine communications job. It also helps explain the pivotal role that lawyers must play.

But this should not mute the company. It does not mean that public relations cannot create in-plant programs to improve the basic economic education of employees (to give them ultimately a better basis for evaluating the money package involved in contract negotiations).

Nor does it mean that every legitimate means cannot be taken to give employees some feeling for the company's progress; its future, its competitive situation and its problems (no one has yet ruled that such information violated labor laws). Today's educated, informed and increasingly sophisticated employees are competent to reach their own decisions, given the facts and arguments of both sides on matters affecting their jobs, pay and job security. Management has, in fact, an obligation to give employees facts bearing on their jobs, including the competitive realities.

The most effective public relations employment, like the preventive medicine concept of Chinese doctors, is that done *before* labor negotiations get under way, or *before* a strike breaks. The issues that bear directly upon most employees' attitudes and actions during a strike—job security, job benefits, working conditions, fringes, pensions, hospitalization—cannot be objectively discussed during the fever of a strike. If the company's position on each point is strong, this has to be brought out in the daily communication with employees months and weeks before negotiations begin. Most industrial relations experts recognize this, and wholeheartedly collaborate with public relations in development of realistic programs to accomplish it. They also have their fingers on the pulse of the plant and can detect possible trouble spots of misunderstanding or uncertainty.

For example, it's not too surprising that employees fear change: a new plant, new machines, a merger and new management. They want reassurance that change does not menace their job security; failing to get this, they are reluctant to accept changes in their work methods and may, ultimately, seek redress—and reassurance—in a strike. Industrial relations and line management may know that the facts are contrary to the rumors, but they need guidance in the business of communicating these facts to the employees. And they get this from the public relations department.

Management policy, the concept of profits, the role of competition, including foreign competitors—these are meaty subjects to educate and inform employees about. They must be told, and told in such a way that an employee will first be interested, and second, will comprehend the essence of each and, hopefully, will accept the facts as they are spelled out. The legal department is not concerned with these issues ex-

127

cept abstractly; its prime involvement is the contract, its implementation and the preparation for the next negotiation. Industrial relations, concerned with the daily administration of the labor contracts, will support in principle any such information program, but can't, generally, give much manpower or expertise to doing the job themselves. Which leaves it to public relations pretty much to get on with the job.

Since there's little dispute about public relations' value here, the freedom to do an effective job is usually forthcoming. The situation becomes touchier when negotiations open, and they reach their most sensitive point when the strike is on. Public relations wants full and candid disclosure; the lawyers think "no comment" is saying a mouthful and line management is caught between the cross-fire of corporate policy, legal censorship and its own sense of involvement with the employees. Oddly enough, public relations can make its biggest contribution by recognizing what it can *not* do, and thereby not adding further pressure to a tense situation, through misguided loyalty to principle.

In general, the considerations that mature public relations management will follow are:

They won't worry about newspaper visibility. Contracts are not negotiated in headlines or in newspaper copy.

They won't try to assume spokesman's role. Although the logical bridge to the press, public relations should offer no opinions nor venture predictions.

They won't over-react. Labor leaders intuitively use "gut" talk; provocative statements that tend to make everything black and white. Don't feel obliged to respond; you can't win this war of words, anyway.

They won't resist the lawyers' counsel. There are a great many semantic booby traps in even the most straightforward communication during a strike. The lawyers can save the public relations man from well-intended but serious communications faux pas.

128

They won't overcommunicate, either by saturating employees with the so-called "real facts" or by trying to match the union, statement by statement, in the press.

They won't try to discredit union leadership (except in extreme cases, and then only if counsel and industrial relations management agree). Inevitably, they are the ones who can do most to sell management's offer to the rank-and-file and even after the settlement, management still faces the necessity to deal with them in its implementation. Scars burned too deeply can result in bitterness and hostility, even after settlement.

On the more constructive side:

They will aid management in communicating its position in simple, easily understood terms and not in the idiom of law.

They will evaluate all communications as to pertinence to the issues as the employees see them, especially those involving offers.

They will establish the machinery needed for fast public response, anticipating physical as well as policy requirements. Mailing lists, duplicating facilities, photography, typewriters, manpower, etc., must be available for off-premise use.

They will furnish background research. Comments by union leadership, some following last settlement and others made during the intervening time, often speak more strongly for the benefits of the last settlement than any company comments can. Effective use can be made of these, if handled skillfully.

They will assume responsibility for briefing the press. The best guarantee management has for fair and equitable treatment in the press is to assure that they fully understand management's position and the issues involved. Initially, this might be accomplished by development of a White Paper and then a briefing session; periodically, management may meet with the press, or issue additional background memorandums.

Following settlement, there is a natural tendency on the

part of management involved—lawyers, industrial relations experts, et al.—to let down at least temporarily. Public relations, because it must constantly consider the long-term viewpoint, cannot; it should immediately map out a program to: fully communicate all aspects of the new collective bargaining contract to employees; consider what interpretations will be given to non-union employees who are as affected by the new contract terms; weigh the merits of communicating the gist of the new settlement to those outside the corporate family, i.e., to customers (if they've been negatively affected by a long plant shutdown) or to stockholders (if it will seriously affect earnings, either by the money package or loss of business during a shutdown); and to other selected opinion leaders whose support and understanding are essential to the continued health of the company.

While many of the issues raised in negotiations are points of strategy and not necessarily to be taken at face value, they often raise subtle questions not resolved by the legal language of the contract. They may, for example, bring out into the open basic and deeply rooted misunderstandings of management or how the company conducts its business. Public relations must be concerned over these aspects. Sometime after everyone's caught up on his sleep, it would be appropriate for public relations to initiate a de-briefing session to assay what's been learned about employee attitude as reflected in the past negotiations. Soft spots of information can be pinpointed and attended to, from an education standpoint. Management may adopt new policies as the result of the settlement and, ultimately, these will have to be communicated and interpreted to employees.

It's been said that you begin negotiating for the next contract the moment the new one is signed. Most industrial relations people and management will accept that; for labor relations today is not a cold war power struggle, with open warfare once every two or three years. It's a long-term effort concerned with establishing the best possible relationships

130

between management and its employees. To the degree that public relations judgments and public relations communication skills represent the best resources that can be applied to aspects of this association, they should be employed.

COMMUNITY RELATIONS

Companies, no less than their individual employees, instinctively want to live in harmony with their neighbors. The community supplies much of the manpower, and through education keeps the pool stocked. It provides municipal services and civic and legislative support, and it sets the tax rate, equitably or punitively, depending to a large extent upon its relationship with its corporate citizens. Too much is at stake to leave this relationship to chance. Deliberate efforts must be made to make it mutually beneficial. This is, obviously, community relations, or plant-city relations, as it is sometimes called.

Some corporate diehards still hold to the obsolete view that good community relations begin and end with a checkbook; give to the local charitable causes and there'll be no interference, and no problems. Newspapers daily record the folly of this old-line, paternalistic view. Communities expect and demand more of their local enterprises than philanthropy; they expect the company to participate fully in the *total* life and well-being of the community. Problems of unemployment, urban sprawl, air and water pollution, taxes, civil rights, education, political leadership, welfare—the list of responsibilities is as long an inventory for a community as it is for the nation as a whole.

In fact, the community is a microcosm of the nation. It's not one homogeneous group of people. It is at least a dozen publics. It is the *education groups,* the school board, teachers, PTA; it's the *professionals,* the clergy, the doctors, dentists, nurses, lawyers, bankers and engineers; it is the *fraternal*

131

members, the Kiwanians, the Rotarians, the Lions, the members of the lodges, veteran groups, women's and garden clubs; it's *business* and *industrial* people, the Chamber of Commerce, the Board of Trade, the merchants and industrialists; it's the *civic leaders,* the politicians, the police and firemen, the judges; it's the *youth,* YMCA, YWCA, YMHA, YWHA, Boy Scouts, Girl Scouts, students; it's the media, the reporters, newscasters, editors and publishers; and it's labor leaders, church leaders, barbers, taxi drivers, postmen and garage mechanics. And when it's all tallied up, it is the *community-at-large,* which may often react differently as a group than its members would individually.

These differing views, attitudes and opinions rarely adopt a laissez-faire posture toward a company. They're opinionated, dogmatic and vociferous about it—and they're not just making noise. They can hinder a company from conducting its business in many ways: through onerous ordinances, difficult zoning regulations and by resisting or unduly drawing out negotiations on any petitions of the company for relief or for action on other matters. They can be of little aid and comfort to the company in times of hot labor dispute or even a strike (withholding sympathy and support). Broadsided public criticism can have not only a deleterious impact on the company's reputation (or image); it can seriously impinge on the attitudes and morale of employees.

Obviously, companies today would no more overlook or neglect their community relations than they would allow their taxes to go unpaid or their insurance policies to lapse. There is, however, a great deal more involved here than assigning the plant management and the public relations representation to "get the word" out about the company where it will do the most good. Sound community relations are not built on rhetoric, or developed through a local information explosion.

It begins with policy decisions. Corporate public relations should be, at the very least, a catalyst here. The decisions start with defining citizensip (the corporate version is not that much different from the individual one) and measuring the company's performance against that standard. The public relations adviser must know the community; if he doesn't he should make it his business to do so under forced draft. Then a balance sheet might be drawn up totaling what the company's involvement with the community is and what the community, for its part, seems to expect from the company and what, in the judgment of those qualified to say, seem to be the community's most pressing needs. What resources the company has to bring to bear on these problems should be weighed and their use employed judiciously. For instance, if there's political lethargy in the community, this doesn't mean that the company should take a partisan stand and promote it. But it can mean that the company takes the initiative to foster more interest in elected government. It has, after all, the resources for holding meetings, for educational material; it can set up speakers' bureaus to stir interest and, of course, it has the core of an opinion-molding group in its own local employees, whether there are a few hundred or several thousand.

Specific objectives of a community relations program differ from company to company, as do the character and makeup of individual companies. But there is one thread common to all objectives: The corporation wants to be known and viewed as a good employer and an asset to the community. Again, self-analysis precedes communication.

Assuming that the corporate house is in reasonable order, public relations can help in the communication effort by counseling local plant management on techniques and how to "tool up." In many instances public relations can assign a staff representative to work directly with the line managers in this program. The size of the community and that of the plant involved will ultimately determine just how sophisticated the communication program is.

Essentially, the corporation reaches the local public in two ways:

By person-to-person contact through speeches, plant tours, meetings with civic leaders, in-plant programs (recreation, vocational training), annual meetings, special events, personal letters, employee contacts, participation in civic affairs, support of education, religion, sponsoring public service events, responding to emergency needs, open houses, ceremonial affairs, etc.;

By use of local media through radio, television, newspaper news; advertising in all; direct mail, circulation of the company newspaper; the annual report, other periodic reports; billboard display, films, brochures, exhibits, displays, theater/sports programs; retail signs.

The company gets a reading on how the community feels:

By person-to-person contact through speeches by local influentials; informal and formal opinion surveys; from forums and discussion groups; from local civic and political leaders direct and via the community grapevine; from labor leaders; from suppliers and local service people; from employees; from reaction to company projects; from the status of the supply of manpower available to it and from the local sale of the company's products;

By local media through editorial comment in newspapers, on radio or over TV; in advertising; through comments on proxy statements of local stockholders; through personal letters, etc.

Public relations will also see to it that local management fully understands the primary rules undergirding a practical communications effort. This is necessary to guarantee that the communications themselves do not sabotage what might otherwise be exemplary planning and programming of community relations.

For example, public relations knows and will emphasize to local management that a businesslike communication program cannot be done part-time, nor can it be delegated to inexperienced employees. If there are no experienced employees, corporate public relations should do what it can to bring this to top management's attention and to find a solution. Further, whatever the means, informal or formal, some consistent effort should be expended to get a feeling of the effectiveness of the communications effort. What sort of two-way flow of information is there? Obviously, a sound community relations program must involve the corporation's own employees; it cannot be a project packaged without their participation. How and when they're brought in is at the discretion of local management, but since it is their company and their community, so it must also be their program, at least portions of it.

This means, too, that regular consideration should be given to plant tours or full-scale open house programs. Nothing adds more impetus to a community relations effort than to give employees an opportunity to show off where they work. Conversely, nothing would be more disastrous than to have management's support of such a program a half-hearted one; there can be no niggling over cost or insisting on restrictions that are more nuisance than legitimate.

Finally, public relations, either local or corporate, would seriously be defaulting on its basic responsibility if it did not have a specific "disaster plan." The elaborateness of such a procedure is again a matter of individual company specifications. But it must anticipate any and all major catastrophes, and cover, in advance, all procedures pertaining to press inquiry, corporate-wide communications, employee fatalities and the mobilization of appropriate emergency services. Of all, communication ultimately becomes the most critical. Theon Wright and Henry S. Evans in their book, *Public Relations and the Line Manager* (American Management Association, 1964), point out that the handling of news coverage and public relations in time of disaster demands professional training and experience. "It cannot be left to the haphazard direction of poorly qualified or overly officious staff executives, or the damage to a company's image may be as serious as the disaster itself."

A 20-page manual of emergency procedures prepared for plant and laboratory managers by Celanese Corporation's public relations department is one of the most succinct and comprehensive outlines developed. In addition to explaining the rationale of emergency plans, it explains how the press should be handled, and why; what they are likely to expect, and how to provide for such things as a press room, press tours of accident site, information sources, the matter of photographs, and how to follow up after the emergency. A novel Calldex phone index is also supplied that gives a handy reference to key plant and headquarter official phone numbers, media phones and an on-the-spot check list of reminders of emergency steps.

While most people are exceedingly tolerant of a company in trouble during a major catastrophe, there is still no escaping the fact that how the company handles itself, publicly, in these periods of stress, as well as in good times, firmly fixes its reputation. Generally, three of its most valued publics are intimately involved: the employees, the community and the local press. Public relations problems can easily arise with any or all of these three groups, unless the situation is anticipated and machinery developed to cope with it.

BUSINESS-GOVERNMENT RELATIONS

Every chief executive officer of every major corporation knows intimately and sometimes despairingly of the ever-widening role government plays in his corporation's life. Government has been called our "biggest growth industry" and even the smallest legislative maneuver is likely to send shock waves through all the neurons of the company's nervous system. Since no corporation of consequence will be ignored by Washington, none can afford to ignore it. And, if business chooses to ignore the more than 2,000 correspondents accredited to use the press facilities of the capital, there are 535 accomplished propagandists who have no such compunctions. Insofar as the members of Congress are concerned, it is an elementary rule of political science that while a public official may not live by publicity alone, no public career is likely to prosper without it.

Where should the responsibility be assigned? Americans believe in numbers, so some executives seek their clues there. There are 2,500 trade associations with Washington offices, so maybe this is the most effective avenue. What about the highly paid, high-powered lobbyists of which so much is written? There are some 1,200 of them, so obviously they have their place and their role. Many corporations leave the matter strictly up to the lawyers, and the 15,000 lawyers in the capital number among their ranks some of the nation's most prestigious legal brains. And, finally, the public relations brethren; there are upwards of 1,000 public relations practitioners in Washington (which is really a puny force when measured against the 6,858 federal employees who, working on a $425 million publicity budget, spend twice as much generating their information, news and views as the nation's two major wire services, the three major networks and the 10 biggest newspapers).

Each, of course, has its role, and it is usually a significant one. Trade associations have the expertise, resources and latent muscle from their clusters of companies; but of course theirs is a view of recognized bias. Professional lobbyists are either extraordinarily effective (the ones who do their homework and are thoroughly prepared), or are members of the three-X club: *ex*troverts who *ex*aggerate their *ex*pertise.

The labyrinthian legal procedures typical of contracts, statutes and administrative regulations make the lawyer a valued resource in Washington, and some accomplish a great deal in representing their client's interests; but lawyers are not communicators.

137

And public relations people are, so the mantle falls to them, right? Wrong!

At least not for the total responsibility. While public relations people congenitally have an appetite for responsibility as boundless as their ambition, the problem in setting up a Washington command post to monitor and mastermind a company's relations with government is simply broader than public relations, per se. A Washington office fundamentally is an information-gathering and judgment-making entity. Granted, there are considerable public relations overtones to detecting and evaluating shifts in public policy, in weighing the human relations element of politics, and in taking the temper of support for such issues as unemployment, decent housing and education for all. But, too, a Washington office has to be on top of—if not ahead of—the waves of intricate legal, statutory, legislative, political, administrative measures that are generated daily.

Consider the volume of just a few of the agencies that generally hold, if not life-and-death, certainly a strategic power over corporations. The FCC is said to process almost 3,000 applications daily; the ICC approves more than 2,000 tariffs and schedules every year; the NLRB disposes of more than 25,000 unfair labor practice charges a year, and the FTC receives and reviews about 800,000 printed advertisements and commercials every year. This is only a modicum of the tidal wave of paperwork disgorged daily by government agencies.

Passage of public bills, which this diagram plots—either "authorization" or "appropriation" bills—may be introduced by a member of the House or by a senator. Revenue bills must originate in the House. Bills, numbered according to the order introduced (starting with No. 1), must be acted upon during the two-year life span of a Congress, or they will have "died." Bills are read twice, numbered, then referred to the committee having jurisdiction over their subject matter. The chairman of the Standing Committee assumes respon-

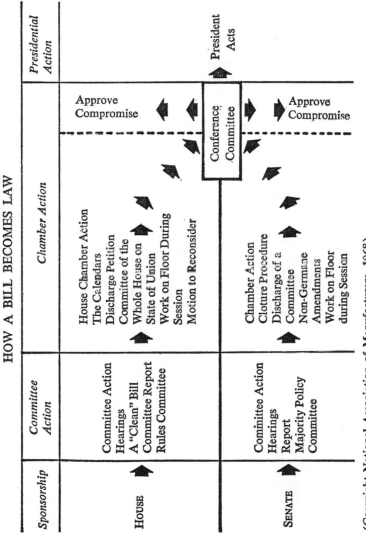

HOW A BILL BECOMES LAW

Sponsorship	Committee Action	Chamber Action		Presidential Action

HOUSE

Committee Action
Hearings
A "Clean" Bill
Committee Report
Rules Committee

House Chamber Action
The Calendars
Discharge Petition
Committee of the
Whole House on
State of Union
Work on Floor During
Session
Motion to Reconsider

Approve
Compromise

Conference
Committee

President
Acts

SENATE

Committee Action
Hearings
Report
Majority Policy
Committee

Chamber Action
Cloture Procedure
Discharge of a
Committee
Non-Germane
Amendments
Work on Floor
during Session

Approve
Compromise

(Copyright National Association of Manufacturers, 1968)

139

sibility for the bill, referring it to a subcommittee, or creating one to handle it; or he can place it immediately before the full committee.

Most major bills get a hearing; testimony from interested parties and experts is presented either in public or closed "executive sessions." If the subcommittee studying fails to take action or reports unfavorably, the bill generally is dead. A favorable report brings the bill to the full committee, which may: pass it along to the House, refuse to, or send it back to the subcommittee. If the revisions, amendments, etc., made before the bill leaves the committee are extensive, the bill is re-drafted, and a "clean bill" re-introduced. Bills reported from a House committee must be accompanied by written reports. The Rules Committee establishes ground rules for House chamber action (i.e., limit debate, accept or not accept amendments, etc.).

There are three regular and several special "calendars" on which the bill may be listed. The procedures for bringing it to vote are intricate. Even then a bill may be rejected by voting it down, tabling it or sending it back (recommit) to the committee with or without instructions, the latter to all intents killing the bill.

Counter-balance to Rules Committee or to any committee withholding action, is right of House member to file motion to "discharge" a committee from role in judging bill and, if upheld, bring bill to immediate consideration. The Senate has virtually the same procedures, with the exception of no rules committee controlling the flow of legislation to the Senate floor. Senate debate on a bill is unlimited unless cloture procedure is invoked (which, by agreement, limits time for discussion). If a committee fails to report on a bill, the Senate may discharge it of its responsibility and put the bill on the calendar. The Senate, in contrast to the House, does not insist that amendments be germane to a bill and they are often added to get action that the bill otherwise would not generate. On the floor, the Senate can vote to:

140

amend the bill, table it, recommit it, pass it, defeat it, or reconsider the passage of any amendment.

Since neither the House nor the Senate is likely to pass identical bills (seldom does a major bill make the Congressional tour without changes being made), a conference is called to act on the differences in the bill as it passed through the two chambers. Conference reports go back to each chamber and, if passed, the bill goes to the President.

He has four possible choices: he can sign it; he can veto it, in which case it goes back to the originating chamber (to override the veto, both the House and Senate must vote to do so); he can fail to act on the bill, in which case, after 10 days, it becomes law; or if Congress adjourns before the 10 days are up, he kills it via the "pocket veto."

Theodore C. Sorenson, formerly special counsel to Presidents Kennedy and Johnson, writing in the *Public Relations Journal* (Vol. XXIV Jan. 1968) pins the responsibility squarely and exclusively on the chief executive officer. It is he and his board of directors and his principal officers, Sorenson says, who must take it upon themselves to know what is going on in Washington—to interest themselves in the policy and political developments and take the initiative to visit with congressmen and senators and with appropriate Cabinet and agency offices. In the final analysis, it is the chief executive of the corporation whose decisions are going to make the difference in business-government relations. And it is these decisions—especially those dealing with the broader social and domestic issues, not the parochial ones of a company or an industry—that have the most telling effect on these relations.

Republican State Senator Edward J. Speno, New York, puts it succinctly: The businessman who fails to stay abreast of the work of the state and federal legislature as it affects his special area of interest is making a serious error. He says the need to live with unworkable and burdensome laws, laws that do not reflect the intelligent point of view and experience

141

of business, could be avoided through simple involvement before the fact rather than after it.

At the state level, Senator Speno cites the advisory committees of joint legislative committees, which draw upon the expertise of business in special areas of interest. This voluntary effort not only brings the talents of business to the lawmakers; it creates the two-way communication vital to the lawmaking process.

The practice of some large corporations of encouraging junior executives and technical people to give part-time service to legislative bodies is not only a public service, Senator Speno says, but a practical means for business to keep apprised of legislation that bears upon its business.

The job of seeing to it that the corporation takes stands that are not always negative, but constructive and reasonable is one involving public relations judgment, but the lawyer, lobbyist and trade association official could make contributions, too, probably in that descending order of impact. Communication of such stands to the proper officials is still another role for the public relations man, although, again not exclusively.

While the massiveness of the government's propaganda machine can easily drown out the timid voice of a company, this in no way means that the media in Washington are cynical journalists whose minds are implacably closed against the business viewpoint. But the company's message has to be said forcefully, factually and at the right time. For example, information revealed for the first time at a formal hearing may make the news, but it probably won't have much effect at the legislative level. Many hearings are really designed by Congress to build support for a position which may already have been arrived at in closed session.

The professional public relations man never forgets his special catechism for communication in Washington. He'll know how to achieve maximum visibility for a point of view and when, how and if to stage a press briefing. He'll make sure that his information is scrupulously objective and accurate. (While it's always disastrous to mislead or misinform the press, in Washington it's hara-kiri.) He'll anticipate questions and will thoroughly know and anticipate the government's point-of-view. If a hearing is involved, he'll see to it that the company's view and the appropriate documentation will be introduced to the committee before deliberations are concluded. Then when the corporate witnesses repeat them publicly at the hearing, he will have made all necessary arrangements to publicize these views far and wide.

Businessmen should not interpret bureaucratic fever as anti-business attitude. The beadledom orientation of much of Washington's officialdom, ruled by inflexible routines, is instinctively reluctant to reopen an issue once it's been disposed of. There's no anti-business prejudice involved; just a resolute tendency to view something finished as finished. Why work it over twice?

Naturally, there are ways to encourage a second look, but it's what is done about communicating the company's view beforehand that really counts. Government decisions are not made in vacuums. They are in response to law and to public opinion. Time after time the lawmakers have openly solicited corporate views, not at the last minute or on a crisis basis, but on something of a regular schedule. Business too often reacts suspiciously, if it responds at all.

What it seems to fail to appreciate is that the tidal wave of bills introduced in each Congress—it's been said it approaches 20,000—simply overwhelms the modest staff assistance available to both majority and minority members of Congress for deep and penetrating research. This increase in Congressional work-load—which has not, incidentally, been matched by appropriate modernization of procedures— understandably minimizes the time that can be given each and every issue for penetrating analysis. Despite the fact that Congress as a group is better informed, better educated, better acquainted with more issues and more responsive to the

143

public's interest than at any time previous, it is interested in business's views; it appreciates and is responsive to factual backgrounding in a complex subject, whether it's weaponry, air pollution or tariff matters.

Sorenson says the most prevalent characteristic of business attitudes toward Washington is complete naïveté. In his years on the Hill he found it a strange paradox that many executives who thoroughly know their way around a balance-sheet and an annual report become completely lost on Capitol Hill.

Even today, despite the seemingly greater participation of business in Washington activity, as witness the nearly 100 business leaders in 150 cities engaged in the National Alliance of Businessmen's attack on poverty and hard-core unemployment, there are many who still could do much to improve their business relations with a modern Congress. Sorenson raised some fundamental do's and don't's at a luncheon meeting in New York for the National Industrial Conference Board two years ago that are no less valuable today.

First, he said, don't always assume the worst—that all liberal lawmakers are anti-business or that no popular bill can be amended. Don't belittle a politician as a "man who never met a payroll." You've never carried a precinct. He also cautions about watering down your effectiveness either by taking on too many fights or by being consistently negative and opposed. Show some of the same energy by being *for* something once in a while.

On the positive side, Sorenson joins in making the universal plea heard in Washington: get in on pertinent legislation at the formative stage, not after the sponsors are committed and their positions are more or less frozen. And if any chief executive officer still harbors doubt as to the reception he'll receive from his own Congressman or Senator, or any other lawmaker for that matter, take to heart this advice from Sorenson:

"Let your own Congressman or Senator, and others as

well, hear directly and personally from you—not only at banquets or meetings, not only to complain, not only when your business needs his vote, not only when he solicits your help or opinion, but also when you have a constructive suggestion on your own, or when he has delivered a particularly thoughtful or courageous view or vote that has nothing to do with your business. And when you do oppose a bill, *do* offer constructive, realistic alternatives or compromise amendments; offer facts and reason, not threats and exaggerated fears; try to understand the sponsor's political motivations, and try to allay instead of confirming his suspicions of yours."

These recommendations may seem patently like good common sense. Of course they are, but it goes a good deal deeper than that. The ground rules for just doing these things—communicating, meeting with lawmakers, briefings, etc.—comprise a modus vivendi all their own, a ritual unique to the environment. Lobbyists, lawyers as well as public relations men, are versed in the routine. The latter, however, may offer some additional dimensions of judgment and perspective. The public relations man is the one generally best-informed on the company's over-all objectives, on its public affairs policies, on its public relations policies (in the broadest definition). He does not tend to specialize in one or a few aspects of the corporation's activity, as a lawyer might in tariff matters or a lobbyist in partisan legislation on taxes.

But this does not mean that the vice president of public relations should be the policy-making administrator of this highly sensitive listening post, unless he reports on his stewardship of it directly to the chief executive. The chief executive officer, who must be the policy-maker for public relations activity and philosophy, must also be the same alter-ego for the Washington operation, if a viable business-government relationship is to develop.

CHAPTER EIGHT

Social Problems, Profits
and Public Relations

Thoughtful business leaders today are well aware that the whole future of their enterprise is inevitably and intimately tied into the community and the world around them. They know that they cannot with wisdom and circumspection plan for the future of their corporations without also determining what contributions they can make to solving the ills of their social environment.

The monumental upheavals in our cities and communities—fed almost hourly by the poisons escaping from urban deterioration, riots and human despair—have created, one observer commented, a social Pearl Harbor. Business has been caught up in the national fever to do something constructive; waves of self-conscious actions ebb and flow throughout the nation as program mounts upon program to correct these metropolitan maladies. But for all of the fervor of this mobilization of resources to stave off Armageddon, many businessmen still harbor secret, possibly subliminal doubts. Is what's best for society in the best interests of the shareholder? Or, conversely, will what's in the best interests of the stockholder adequately serve the interests of society?

Can a corporation really justify using the stockholder's money to solve social problems, on the excuse that this would produce a better environment in which to sell more goods?

146

Social Problems, Profits and Public Relations

Can do-gooding be profitable as well as charitable? Need it be?

These are typical of the flinty questions business must habitually ask itself. They are the kind any good public relations man would anticipate and be prepared to guide management to the right answers. They deserve pragmatic, not theoretical, answers.

Flatly, the answer to these questions is Yes. And public relations should have no difficulty articulating its position.

Public relations is not, let us be clear on this point, the all-wise seer of any corporation on this troublesome challenge. But there are specific occupational practices that put public relations in a better over-all position to develop the most practical perspective. The questions that all managements face is, "What constitutes proper social responsibility on the part of a corporation?" "What can my company do?" Public relations, trained to look at all the facets of any problem, has the background as well as the insight into the corporation's long-range ambitions to put any such actions into the right focus. Dealing as it must almost exclusively with people, their attitudes and reactions, public relations has both the technical skills and the intangible qualities of judgment critically needed in support of such programs.

It is not a match-up between profits and social welfare. Any public relations adviser worth his salt will point out that this is a specious riddle. What's more to the point is that the profit system itself is on trial, because, as Charles Y. Lazarus, president of F. & R. Lazarus & Co., pointed out in a speech earlier in 1968, we shall either adapt to meet the needs of the people, or the people, in Government, will change our system for us, including the profit system itself.

Actually, our motives—as they should be in our system of free enterprise—can be economic as well as social. In the opinion of Westinghouse Electric's president, Donald C. Burnham, these broad problems ultimately offer opportunity for growth and profit as industry stirs its entire enterprise to solving them. Henry Ford II thinks that the experience of the past few years makes quite obvious the connection between the pursuit of profit and the public welfare.

Public relations, in the context of this civil struggle, can and should be the stable base serving as a firm foundation for the origin and execution of social programs. There should be no question of unanimity in the corporation on the need— simply a question of what and how. One could say the same of the citizenship exercising its right to vote, but the absentee rate still runs high. It is not unusual to find that the subject of what constitutes the corporation's specific role in exercising its social responsibility generates as many gusts of irrational emotion within the corporate family as it does in the charged ghetto atmospheres.

PERSPECTIVE BEFORE SOCIAL ACTION

To take the extreme view, management choice can polarize. The chief executive can choose to turn his full organization over to an all-out, no-holds-barred campaign on hard-core unemployment, welfare, public education, housing, crime, congestion, birth control and civil rights. But stockholders who see their nest eggs withering may ask him to get more deeply involved as one of the (trained) unemployed. On the other hand, management can look for "safe" social issues to solve; milk for the local kindergarten children; parking facilities to ease Main Street shopping and, of course, modest contributions to all charities around. However, neither the community nor the stockholders are likely to be impressed by this wishy-washy leadership.

Management needs perspective—public relations-oriented perspective. And management should get it without asking for it from his specialist in these areas. This is not an "either or" choice; there is no incompatibility between the

need of his enterprise to show a profit and the obvious need
it has to serve society in some practical manner.

If the chief executive were planning the introduction of
a new product, or setting the stage for a major policy change,
there'd be no question of how the organization would be
efficiently mobilized. Its various resources—sales, marketing,
research, engineering, production, line management—would
be briefed and coordinated. Targets and objectives would be
identified, analyzed and computerized and the logistics set,
and smoothly the wheels would turn.

Business can be, even though it often is not, as sure-
handed about solving its sociological problems. Perhaps it's
the riots, violence and other eruptions of the super-heated
emotions that encourage management to think differently and
less confidently about these new problems. The public relations man is the one who should keep his cool. He should
be in the front ranks, but as a catalyst, not as a crusader.

He recognizes and will counsel management that business
alone, especially one company, cannot solve all of the social
problems, so he won't let the magnitude of the challenge
overwhelm the corporation. For all of its innovative talent
and management skills, business can't singlehandedly eradi-
cate illiteracy of 3 million people fourteen years old or older;
it can't rehabilitate all of the substandard housing, find jobs
for the 3 million unemployed, eliminate crime in the streets,
or underwrite college educations for all the nation's youth.
But no one business has a key to do the job by itself.

The wise public relations man will curb his own ambitions as well as any tendency on the part of his company
to over-react. This is not an abnormal tendency. As a matter
of fact, urbanologist Daniel P. Moynihan says that it's an
American fault to insist on extravagant goals, as if to set out
to achieve anything less than everything suggests a lack of
sincerity. As a result, he says, the social history of the '60s
is already littered with the wreckage of crash programs that

were going to change everything and, in fact, changed nothing.

So, the counsel that public relations gives in this new arena for the corporation must be practical. This may seem trite; common sense doesn't perhaps shape up as a very dramatic tool with which to tackle problems like those reflected in the riots of Watts, Newark, Kansas City and Washington, D.C. Common sense, in case anyone needs reminding, is also reflected in good employee relations, stockholder relations, labor relations, etc. Yet, despite its universal application, other specialists are still required: lawyers, financial specialists, industrial relations experts and public relations people. Let us not therefore distort, becloud or belittle public relations' impact and contribution simply because it begins, as it always must, with common sense. Half of the public relations skill applied here is spent in helping management decide what to do and when to do it, the other half in investing the execution with the necessary professionalism.

Basically this means matching resources to the community's needs. It means creating a partnership with local government. It means anticipating a slackening in dedication after the initial crisis is passed, and developing means and methods to prevent inertia from stagnating the project. And it means a continuous discussion within the corporation of this new activity, so that it becomes, not a one-time emergency project, but part and parcel of everyday planning.

The high degree of visibility to which the public relations adviser is subject as he performs his duties does not mean that public relations is a façade behind which management can undisturbedly run its business as before. Management can delegate the chores and mechanics of such programs, but it cannot escape the need for deep personal involvement. It takes more than the mere authorization of some enlightened measures to convince the community that a corporation is really aware of, and is trying to measure up to, its responsibilities. The community wants evidence that the top executive *is* involved. Because, if there's one additional emotional

150

characteristic of the mob's mood of anger, frustration and despair, it is cynicism. People have to be persuaded that the steps any corporation is taking are tangible and sincere developments, realistically within its means, and not publicity ploys.

In a very real sense, the chief executive is the field general of this action. It doesn't require personal exposure to violence or riots. But it does mean some first-hand involvement in the analysis of the problems, in the planning of the remedial action, in the weighing and measuring of the results and in the determination of what new inputs are required. There's nothing revolutionary in this. The precedent has been set. For it was under the leadership of the chief executives that the following programs were created and executed:

Armstrong Cork: Renovated buildings for low- and moderate-income families in Lancaster, Pa.; *Chrysler:* Adopted a "buddy" system, pairing disadvantaged new employees to make them more comfortable, and help them on their jobs; *Ford:* Hired nearly 2,000 "hard-core" unemployed persons in employment centers established in inner city areas, providing bus and lunch money prior to initial paychecks; *General Electric:* Installed, in cooperation with Philadelphia, an automated crime detection and reporting system and is developing a similar system in Syracuse, N.Y.; *Inland Steel:* Following initiation of a weekly TV show broadcasting job opportunities, in cooperation with CBS, 3,000 people were placed in the first five weeks; *Koppers:* Cooperated with 20 other companies to form a corporation to purchase and rehabilitate vacant, condemned homes and to sell them for $10–$12,000.

Also, *Michigan Bell Telephone:* In conjunction with a city high school, teaches Detroit students how to get jobs, providing them also with the job skills needed to hold the jobs they secure; *Montgomery Ward:* 25 of its employees work with the Chicago Housing Authority one evening each week tutoring disadvantaged tenants in basic reading skills; *PPG Industries:* Through the PPG Foundation, will grant

151

scholarships to provide 100 policemen with training degrees in police science; *Raytheon:* Provides six company specialists in physics, chemistry, mathematics and astronomy to advise and assist teachers, counsel guidance personnel on employment openings and standards, and improve curricula in Boston's public schools; *Woolworth:* Plans to open the second-largest of its New York City stores in Harlem.

It is no coincidence that the National Alliance of Business comprises 15 corporate presidents and chief executives from such nationally known companies as Ford, Coca-Cola, I.T.T., Aluminum Company, Hotel Corporation of America, Mobil Oil, McDonnell Douglas, Ling Temco, Illinois Bell, and Levi Straus. Further, business executives in 50 cities have served as supervisors of the National Association of Manufacturers' program to hire a half-million hard-core unemployables under its new National Alliance of Businessmen project.

IS PUBLICITY TABOO

Now, while there is a clear distinction between image and substance in this arena of social activity, it does not mean there's a prohibition on communicating an enterprise's efforts. In fact, there is every justification for according this activity some priority, although it must be handled with unusual circumspection and skill.

Bear in mind that a prime consideration motivating action in this social field is the realization that companies cannot operate, profitably or otherwise, unless they have public acceptance. Further, the public must believe that the corporation is using its initiative, creating skills and physical reserves in behalf of the national good. Therefore, when business does put its money where its mouth is, it should not be embarrassed to let others see and know it.

It would, of course, be as misguided to brag about such

action as it would be to decline to take credit for it. Too often, non-professionals jump to the conclusion that this is a yes-or-no publicity decision and in that context they invariably equate publicity with new product press-agentry. To debate that is to argue technique, when what should be reviewed is the basic philosophy.

The communication aspects and needs of corporate involvement in social problems are every bit as important as the communications with any of the familiar publics with whom every enterprise deals. No public relations professional can divorce himself from the self-assigned responsibility of seeing to it that this need is satisfied. Conventional procedures for setting up the machinery for such communication may not be adequate here. For example, great care must be taken that any statements published will not be vulnerable to indignant attack by even the more volatile leaders of the community's minority groups. How a unanimity is achieved in advance is, naturally, a difficult question, but the public relations adviser will find the answer, because he knows he must. More often than not, joint announcements, joint briefings or press conferences offer an equitable solution. Corporations should probably underplay rather than overemphasize their role; again, it's a matter of individual judgments.

However difficult and tricky this communication effort is, there is no escaping the fact that the community must be made aware of the activities of the company. In addition to the obvious merits of keeping people informed, heavy publicity is needed in some cases to get a program off the ground. Take the matter of training hard-core unemployables. Such a program may have to be publicized extensively just to encourage these men and women to show up for the training.

It is particularly necessary, of course, to get reliable feedback of how the program is progressing—what the community thinks of it, what the participants think of it, and what needs revamping, beefing-up and so on. This is the kind of inquiry that's basic public relations procedure, so the executive in charge of public relations should need no prompting to arrange for a satisfactory inflow of intelligence.

Everyone looks at such information as is gathered in this process from his own point of view. For example, take a program of training unskilled employees—perhaps from the ranks of the hard-core unemployable. Engineering would be concerned about how the items being made hold up in use. Production would worry about the care and maintenance of the machines used by the unskilled trainees. Financial's concern is cost. Marketing's the impact, if any, on the company's quality image. These parochial views are normal. But, *only* top management and public relations feel primarily obligated to worry about the human opinions expressed, the way they are expressed and what attitudes are conveyed to the community, how widespread they are, and what the implications for the company are in terms of long-term growth and success.

A CREDIBILITY TEST

If the people living in our ghettos find it difficult to accept as real the suggestion that anyone is actually going to help them, they have cause to be skeptical. Thirty-five years ago, the first Presidential Commission was formed on urban problems. If the verbiage of all the committees, seminars and conventions on the subject that have since proliferated were laid out flat, it would probably make a two-lane highway from Newark to Watts and back again. The highway would be paved with definitions and goals but precious little concrete would be found in the way of methods to achieve these goals.

So whatever business attempts it will face a severe credibility hurdle, and no one knows this better than an informed public relations adviser.

What does this mean to him and his company's programs? Simply this:

One, he'll have to concentrate on generating interest and action within his company before he authorizes or creates any public statements on the subject. He will give short shrift to "me-too" speeches; in fact, he'll embargo them. They'll only inflame the hotheads and fuel the charges of the skeptics.

Two, he'll make certain that his corporation's investment is realistic, and that management itself has a realistic view of the investment. The only profits involved are those of survival as a quality organization, which may be too abstract for immediate comprehension, so there's some internal education necessary, too.

Three, he'll play "devil's advocate" and question, if need be, the irrelevant in an area where unemployment is nil; likewise support of higher education is commendable, but academic, if the university's in the next county seat.

Four, and here he treads on dangerous ground, he'll feel obligated to challenge the adequacy of the proposed program. It can't be a minimal or token effort, just to get on the books. Obviously there's no hard and fast rule that so many thousands or even millions have to be invested. But it must be of enough substance to guarantee that something tangible will come of it.

Five, and finally, the public relations executive will, by his own means of internal communication and/or education, prepare management for disappointment in the feedback it will get on its program. One of the biggest mistakes we can make when companies get involved in the kind of change we're having in our society, according to Dr. Raymond Mack, professor of sociology at Northwestern University and urban consultant to Carl Byoir & Associates, is to expect gratitude. We are inclined to think, he says, that the Negro we hire for that job ought to be grateful to us for doing this, because we didn't used to do it. Dr. Mack doesn't agree. He reminds

155

us that people don't feel obliged to be grateful upon getting something they think they deserved all along and had been deprived of.

The public relations man knows this and tries to condition his management to it, primarily so that it does not despair and throw in the towel.

As was stated, common sense covers a lot of ground: credibility, for example, if the public relations man is there to do the almost always necessary prodding.

CHAPTER NINE

How to Talk with, and Work with Public Relations (And Get the Most from It)

Nothing is more expensive today for a corporation than mediocre public relations. It shortchanges a company on its present investment and it steals from its future. The added strain on management and the energy it is obliged to expend to cope with the inevitable problems arising with its publics—problems that are, of course, as inescapable as taxes—are the most recognizable penalties. Harder to measure is the forfeiture of "what might have been"—the intangibles that a creative public relations program would have sensed, identified and somehow translated into the dynamic, positive action that management already attributes to itself.

Mediocre public relations is appeasement public relations. It is safe, accustomed, conventional, and non-controversial. It measures the year's performance by the tranquility it fosters, inflating this placidness as a sign of strength.

If anything, it's a sign of fraud! It's a philosophy predicated on a counterfeit premise, i.e., that public relations' job is to keep things serene and on even keel. What's spurious about this reasoning is that every corporation changes, hourly, monthly, annually. Its fundamental principle of existence, to grow and generate profits, is a direct challenge to the status quo. Growth means development, expansion, gradual increase and, above all, change. Public relations, more than any other

157

facet of management except top management itself, must also be dedicated to change.

How does one convert mediocre to excellent? Can the thin public relations operation be fattened up with implants of creativity? Or is an entirely new form needed?

What is the answer? An easy out is to pin the program's shortcomings on the meager capabilities of the incumbent. After all, he hasn't had an original idea since he switched from starched front shirts. But maybe he *did* have many creative ideas—once. Maybe constant "no's" and the pressure of the corporate social structure and the ceaseless erosion of any status and posture he might have had just simply wore him down into the civil service mentality he now exhibits.

In short, mediocre public relations may be management's fault as much as, if not more, than the office holder's. Regrettable as this is, it, too, is understandable. Creative people often are baffling to top management. They don't fit into any norm. They're not necessarily tractable. Public relations, itself, seems transparently simple; it's a matter of making the right judgments and publicizing them. But, as we've seen, neither of these two basic acts—the decision and the communication—are that routine. What might seem like the right judgment for the corporation, such as deciding to build and automate a new plant, can be a public relations disaster in the community (fear of job loss, for one thing) and the communication job becomes a delicate and difficult assignment.

Ideally, the public relations adviser and the chief executive will function as one. Ideally a rapport grows quickly between them, this understanding giving each an intuitive appreciation of the other's role and responsibility. More often than not, though, this relationship has to be constructed, and the building process is a long and evolutionary one with many misunderstandings, prejudices and dogmatic opinions to be overcome.

158

The previous eight chapters spell out what should and should not be expected of a competent public relations adviser. These are concrete guidelines to specific activity. But they'll be effective only in a corporate climate that encourages their use.

Management's role for this part of the association is not easily diagrammed. How does one talk to and work with public relations? It's a subtle and complex art that must be learned through practical experience. To advance a formula would be like trying to blueprint someone else's courtship. Still, logic never inhibits the giving of advice, so from the public relations man's view, here are some pointers that may lessen the debilitating frustrations (to the public relations man) of practicing this counseling art in modern business.

TEN RULES FOR THE CHIEF EXECUTIVE

The talk about a favorable climate does not mean perfect working conditions. It means an environment that offers a high degree of stimulation, which of course comes from the people, not the physical plant. Highly creative and talented people are attracted to a company that has a strong point of view and is willing to fight for it; a company that gives more than lip service to the textbook maxims for planning for growth and progress; that encourages initiative and welcomes rather than fears change. Harold W. Sweatt, honorary chairman of Honeywell, defined the intangibles of his company in four words, "the spirit of restlessness," an elusive something that unquestionably underlies its growth from a modest maker of thermostats to a billion-dollar corporation. Walter W. Finke, who took over a moribund Dictaphone Corporation, created a sense of urgency as he set out to infuse the fine old-line company with a new feeling of dynamism designed to remove any traces of complacency and self-satisfaction. In 1967, his first year, he increased sales 43 per cent and sent

159

earnings soaring to the highest point in the company's 87-year history.

But business is not a cult of personalities; chief executives are not always inspirational leaders who can easily articulate the tenuous qualities driving the corporation. Do not misconstrue the message here. The climate that stimulates effective public relation's activity turns on the little things, too. It does not flourish only in dynamic environments. Some of public relations men's criteria may hardly seem monumental to their chief executives, but if not understood or missed, can have a crushing effect on the creative psyche of the public relations person, on his (or her) dedication, initiative, and just plain eagerness to do more than is asked for.

What are these majestic qualities of behavior that send spirits soaring or plunging with equal ease? Any attempt to codify them would necessarily be arbitrary; nevertheless public relations people do look for and respond to some ten identifiable factors of personal conduct.

1. *Consistency*. Creative people, like public relations practitioners, need a solid, firmly oriented foundation for their planning. They look to management for this consistency of purpose. They can absorb new challenges around-the-clock if there is no vacillation on objectives. Once their objectives are set they become part of the subconscious of public relations people; their thinking (and sometimes dreaming) hours are pointed toward these goals. Any flip-flopping or wavering on these goals represents to them a lack of conviction and erodes the confidence the public relations people have in the first place about the integrity behind them. Management that is predictable and consistent is as vital to the public relations man as blueprints are to an engineer. It enables him to operate from a set of logical principles, to develop long-range plans, and to build consistency into his own programs. This does not mean that objectives and goals

are sacrosanct. But if they're changed or modified it should not be a daily or weekly event.

2. *Criticism.* Public relations people are not perfect. Theirs is an inexact science to begin with. Every program will have some hole in it, some facet of it that is based on largely subjective opinion, and suspect. Don't look for what's wrong with your public relations program; look first for the positive aspects. Don't frame all responses with the "yes, but" formula. By doing this you ultimately set up a hostile air that will keep any good ideas you may have from filtering in. Keep your criticism constructive. This is easier to say than to execute. You have to remember that too big a dose of criticism can destroy confidence, cooperativeness and creativity—the three C's whose loss would seriously weaken any public relations program.

3. *Free Ideas.* Creative people respond enthusiastically to a good new idea, regardless of the author. But their equilibrium is disturbed by an overabundance of ideas from the boss, which soon assume the stature of requirements rather than recommendations. There is obviously more to problem-solving than just an idea, or what seems to be one. The public relations man has to crank into the judgment machinery many factors, few of which the chief executive is competent to evaluate. For example, external reception to the idea; is it credible? etc? A suggestion now and then is always welcome; ideas that carry forward into greater depth a concept advanced by public relations are even more warmly accepted. But a blizzard of amateur brainstorms can ruin the initiative of the public relations people. Further, if you find it necessary to do the thinking for them, assuming that your ideas are more than a self-indulgence, you have a more serious problem. Obviously there's a shortage of talent that you cannot personally fill satisfactorily. A personnel change is in order.

4. *Amateur Editors.* This is more or less a piggyback on the one above; for some reason executives feel an irre-

sistible urge to play city editor when they read copy from their public relations people. Assuming, again, that the public relations person has the professional credentials of a writer, then let him do it. Confine your editing to policy points— factual ones if necessary—but do not pass judgment on headlines, sentence structure, grammar and so on. After all, writing expert Rudolph Flesch says that businessmen are no great shakes as writers themselves. As a matter of fact, he says, there's been a progressive decay of corporate prose. Gobbledygook and business jargon stem from the same roots as air pollution, traffic jams and slums—they're the product of modern civilization. Or as ad man David Ogilvy once said, "Why buy a dog and then bark yourself?" So, leave the writing to us (the public relation'ers).

5. *Penny Ante Mentality*. Because public relations deals so extensively with intangibles, some executives have apparently gotten the idea that it can also subsist on intangibles. 'Tain't so. This is a penny ante attitude. You get results out of public relations in proportion to what you put into it, and this applies to money, as well as to manpower and method. It is not a question of money's not being a critical factor; economies and priorities must exist here as well as elsewhere. But grudging approvals of even the most minute expenditures will soon dry up initiative and you'll have a drone, not a doer on your hands. This applies especially to constant heckling about budgets already approved, as though management regrets the decision and is looking for ways to recoup the commitment. And, if your public relations man comes up with a corking good idea pertinent to some problem at hand, and which is not provided for even in the contingency budget, give him the vote of confidence a straightforward green light represents. It'll pay long-term dividends in performance, that you'll never get through stinginess!

6. *Second-class Citizenship*. To be truly effective, public relations must be involved *before* decisions affecting a corporation's various publics are locked in. This means easy

access and entry of the public relations man to policy levels. Don't shut him off from this access under some false sense of executive privacy. To be repeatedly made aware through little, subtle and insidious means that he's not a member of the executive suite is not only unnecessary but it's likely to make him wonder if you're trying to buy public relations like printing—no involvement, just pay the bills. Public relations people have their idiosyncrasies; perhaps one is that they must feel their work *is* important and that management legitimately cares and tries to work in an open, enlightened manner. They don't worry about being part of the inner circle. But public relations people do feel keenly that their exclusion from policy-making sessions puts their function in the category of an afterthought or as first aid, neither of which will endear you to them, and which will ultimately drive away talented people.

7. *Habitual No'er.* You can't say no forever, although some management people regularly turn their backs and their minds on their own creations. They establish public relations, provide for budget and manpower and set objectives. Then, as if the job is completed, they promptly reject idea after idea, program after program—all for what seem to them to be valid reasons. Could it be, instead, that they can adopt the concept (of public relations) but are afraid to accept the deed because success can never be guaranteed? New ideas, fresh ideas, aggressive programs can be difficult to embrace if you have no courage of conviction; you could, of course, be criticized by the board and the stockholders if it failed. But the penalty may be even more severe if you default on these executive adventures. Public relations people have a higher patience quotient than they are given credit for. But they cannot endure frustration without surcease. Long hours and weekends of work are meaningless without the challenge of a program and the stimulation success brings with it. A constant no'er will soon be surrounded like Noah with only the lower classes of animal life, public relations-wise.

163

8. *A Too-busy Procrastinator*. This is a spin-off of the "no"-addicted executive, and while less fundamentally negative, is even more frustrating and debilitating, because it's like trying to bottle fog. Public relations doesn't even get a flat "no" to cope with; just a series of promises and vague hints that "we'll get down to cases" just as soon as some always mysterious "other" actions are taken. By initially approving a public relations program, you don't, as management, buy a year's freedom from care and involvement. Remember, you *are* the chief executive officer of public relations; no matter how you dodge and take evasive action, that is still your responsibility. Set aside a definite time each day, week or month to discuss the public relations program with your expert. Don't expect him to capture either the feeling or the facts of what you want done by osmosis.

9. *Enthusiasm*. Don't be afraid to show it, if you feel it. Public relations people, like most human beings, react favorably to applause; not that given grudgingly, but that given with animation and enthusiasm. You're not going to spoil them by giving credit where it's due. They live for this approbation. A whoop of approval now and then, a hurrah occasionally, make it all worthwhile and off they go with batteries recharged. You've shown not only awareness of what they've done, but appreciation and understanding of what their creative effort is all about.

10. *Consideration*. Few corporate functions are so conditioned to 24-hour service as public relations is. It is a service arm of the company, and cannot, technically, lock its responsibility in the desk drawer at five o'clock. But don't abuse this availability. Don't make emergencies where none exist, like sending the public relations staff running to the local paper to get the first of the morning editions for some personal or otherwise unimportant item. Also, appreciate the fact that stories cannot be spewed out by rote, as a computer disgorges data. The corporate statements also are limited by the speed limits that human skills at typing, duplication

and collating can impose. Show some appreciation of these facts, and your public relations people will be responsive.

Some—or all—of these little comments on not-so-perfect corporate behavior may raise some hackles. They are not fictitious. But the picture is improving steadily. Management consultant Robert C. Garretson, of Heidrick and Struggles, who's been closely involved in executive "searches" for public relations executives, believes that corporate executives are becoming more definite about what they expect from public relations as they increasingly realize and accept the important responsibilities they personally have to their community and society as a whole. Philosophically, as well as technically, they are looking to their public relations executives to work with them to carry out programs. The word "with" is the key, not on behalf of them necessarily, but *with* them. It sets the right tone for mutual activity.

Nonetheless, many, many executives still treat public relations involvement the way they do religion: They join the church but rarely attend.

CHAPTER TEN

The Feedback: How to Evaluate
and Measure Public Relations

The Achilles heel of many a public relations operation is the weak feedback of results to management. What tangible evidence is accumulated (i.e., newspaper and magazine clippings) seems to be puny documentation of the worth of a major investment such as public relations. Such reports as are made often leave a lot to be desired; we have the unhappy paradox of skilled communicators being unable to translate to their own management the value of their own work.

This is a fundamental flaw—and it need not be.

There is a definite schizophrenic character to public relations reviews, reports and presentations that may dismay, delight or disillusion management, depending upon its level of public relations sophistication. It is often true that those who are most articulate, convincing and erudite in their presentations are those who've done the most superficial job. On the other hand, those with the greatest experience and broadest practical knowledge of the business chalk up the most creditable record of accomplishment, yet tend to be modest to the point of being inept in translating this to management. Perhaps they are too worn out from doing the work to be able to apply the same imagination and energy to merchandising it. More likely, in their personal order of priority, personal merchandising is far down the list; doing the job immediately at hand gets the emphasis.

166

Management, therefore, can reach one of two erroneous conclusions from these disparate reports: One, that public relations is all talk and no real action; or two, that public relations is a routine, one-dimensional proposition (newspaper clippings probably being the prime evidence of activity) that somewhat unimaginatively makes the best of the conditions it inherits.

REPORTS BASIC

Conscientiousness is commendable but no public relations executive can dismiss the importance of adequate internal reporting on the basis of being too busy to take bows. This is noble—and nonsense. First of all, reporting is as much a part of the job as status reports, interim reports, and year-end reviews are part of the daily life of engineering, sales, manufacturing and any other major corporate activity.

Further, denying management regular opportunities to concentrate on the problems and the programs of public relations probably acts as a built-in governor on the growth and development of the program itself. Management has to get its teeth into public relations work to fully understand and appreciate the operational style peculiar to this art, and on such awareness are built broader, more ambitious programs. This rapport does not come by telepathy.

Reporting procedures vary as do companies. Public relations management should plan no fewer than two formal major reports; four would be better. Included should be the initial program for the year, then quarterly interim reports (or a six-month review) and a year-end review, which will logically lead into the next year's program outline. The number of informal reports should have no set limit, the only criterion being pertinence. These will be discussed later.

In the formal reports management should look for—and public relations should provide adherence to—good management practices. Objectives must be clearly and specifically stated. They must be realistic and not over-promise—no grandiose predictions implying a guarantee of success. Jargon has no place in the language of such reports, either. Management isn't familiar with the vernacular of the communications media, and there's no reason it should be.

With objectives detailed, the report should delineate how the public relations organization will be deployed to accomplish them. What kind of timetable will be set? Are the budget allocations realistic? Does it *involve* various departments of the company or is it set up as a self-sufficient operation all its own (which is a danger sign)? These are just some of the questions that management has every justification to expect to find answered in any public relations report. As was pointed out earlier in the chapter on budgeting, there is no excuse for defaulting on detail here either.

An interim report will be more of a hybrid; it will cover both projections and activity to date; or to put it another way, a smorgasbord of past, present and future. It need not be overbearingly lengthy; verbiage can be sacrificed for facts. Certainly it should give management a feel of the tone of activities, where the problems have been, what's been done to solve or minimize these and what constructive actions have been initiated. Logically, the report should be candid about the prospects for completing all assignments by the fiscal year's end.

It may seem negative, but a key factor in such reports is to discuss what *failed,* for whatever reason. Public relations people have as little stomach, generally, as most staff people have for dwelling on the non-successes; nevertheless, this area of attention has particular, and perhaps unique, pertinence. Often the most valuable lessons learned are those wrung out in a critique on what went wrong. It's the sort of object lesson that transforms abstract considerations into tangibles that can be more easily understood.

Consider this hypothetical example. Company A has

undertaken a major program to communicate a new sales policy recently adopted—one that upholds fair trade where legally applicable. Initially, this news falls on pretty deaf ears. The newspapers and trade publications were profoundly uninterested. Why? Was it because the statement, which of necessity had inputs from the legal staff and others concerned with policy, might have been less than clear? Perhaps it shouldn't have been released over the weekend, an action that public relations had counseled against. Of course it was next to impossible to pin down what this move might cost the company initially in lost business. Public relations is always looking for numbers to quote. But there's no gainsaying the fact that the editors obviously didn't attribute any significance to this move, so perhaps a price tag, however qualified, would have helped them put it into focus. It's one thing to say you're going to fair trade your products; it's quite another to say that you are prepared to take an annual $XX-million loss in potential orders to put teeth in your program.

This sort of problem—the match-up among policy, need for communication, and professionals versus non-professionals—comes daily to public relations in many guises and under many flags. What's central to the question is that repeat business of the same nature can often be headed off by frank and candid discussions of the facts. The debriefing character of many public relations reporting or review sessions can easily be a beneficial working session. It should not be a sterile, one-way lecture by the public relations executive.

ANNUAL AND 'OTHER' REPORTS

It is apparent that for the foreseeable future public relations has to educate equally as much as it has to execute, which means that its internal priorities to inform all members of the corporate family of its activities have never been higher. Public relations, articulated as policy, has a pious, sermon-like tone to it. It becomes real and practical only when examples of such conduct are given. Unfortunately this internal education program often takes an inordinate amount of time—time needed elsewhere.

Nevertheless, it is a commitment. So, public relations, without formal requests from management, will generate reports and presentations as often as a project or an activity justifies it. It is not mandated that these all be across-the-board, either. A typical presentation might be the publicity results on a new product recently introduced. The breadth of editorial coverage will be pleasing to sales management, interesting to management, but to the salesmen in the field it may be the first indication they've had (in their personal terms) of the capability of public relations. On the other hand, editorials and mail supporting the company's multi-million dollar investment in an anti-water pollution system may be of interest to all employees, of special interest to the management echelons, and possibly to the stockholders. Some companies make it a practice to have public relations periodically send their salesmen assortments of recent releases, simply to give them a feeling of involvement, and of knowing what's going on in the company. In other cases, special projects, community days, VIP visitations, or field trips for financial analysts have been wrapped up in special reports for selected audiences. Whatever the form, whatever the occasion, the name of the game of communication is "consistency and regularity"—it is far better to find legitimate opportunities to do as much of this as is feasible throughout the year and not wait for an elaborate one-shot at the year's end—the annual review.

But this does not put the annual report in disfavor. To the contrary, many imaginative public relations departments have effectively adopted corporate management's own reporting techniques. Republic Aviation turned out a 26-page annual report that sandwiched in between an outline of the past year's objectives and the upcoming year's objectives, a graphic profile of diversified activity under such headings as: product support; divisional activity; research and development; international relations; community relations; financial relations; advertising; supplier relations and general corporate activities. On other occasions the company's public relations department made its annual review in a 16-minute sound film, in a special edition of the company newspaper, and in an easel visual aid-propped presentation.

Last year, Liberty Mutual's public relations department put its annual report, called "The Leading Edge" to work for it as a prime educational tool. Editorially, in what would constitute the president's letter in corporate reports, it examined current social and economic trends and related their impact on the company and its public relations philosophy and conduct. It charted no easy course for the company, pointing out that a more sophisticated, articulate and demanding consumer and a new world of communication techniques will demand greater flexibility and a new sense of leadership and resourcefulness for devising greater insurance capacity. The 16-page report, as professionally—if not as expensively—done as most corporate annual reports, then reviewed such public relations conceived and managed activities as highway safety, insurance education, public affairs, employee communication, and branch office public relations support.

Robert Lane, Goodyear's public relations vice president, says that while he still programs on an annual basis, formal reports to top management are not limited to the same schedule. As a practical matter, his department communicates its efforts on a daily basis, which is to say that they are always working with some echelon of management on activities. They also make reports on a project basis, and twice over the past three years, the department has made a formal report to the board of directors. On a quarterly schedule, reviews are held with the vice president or general manager of each of the rubber company's 16 divisions or subsidiaries. "We consider our divisions and subsidiaries as clients, and we go at the job of servicing them as though we were dependent on a contract renewal each year," Lane explains.

The epitome of this sort of motivation is exemplified by General Electric's news bureau. Established 40 years ago, as part of the advertising and sales promotion department, its purpose is to serve any GE division or department wishing to promote a product or activity. If it undertook the assignment, the news bureau billed back to the division for the activity. The GE division is not obliged to use the news bureau; they can opt to hire an outside agency. Since it has to, in fact, compete like any outside agency, the news bureau, earlier this year, asked for and received permission to solicit outside, non-competitive (with GE) business as an agency in its own right. This is an interesting experiment, but for all the conscientiousness the autonomy of the news bureau implies, it does not suggest a trend for such internal operations.

To sum up, some examples of reporting techniques are:

Monthly news reports, with highlighted clipping results;

Periodic story inventories circulated to management (no clips);

Special project reports and summaries;

Annual public relations reports (booklet form);

Annual public relations reports (film);

Annual public relations reports (special edition, company newspaper);

Utilization of material prepared for external use, directed internally—fact sheets and corporate profile easels;

Easel presentations for one man, the company president;

Easel presentations for company executive committee;

Special marketing presentations for sales groups.

Some of the reporting occasions:

Upon completion of a major assignment, i.e., plant dedication;

Quarterly, in line with other internal divisions;

Monthly public relations policy meetings can be scheduled;

At annual sales meetings;

As part of departmental projections, generally prior to budget evaluations;

Executive résumé of activities/news of the company following vacation period or summer plant shutdown, or whatever the local case may be.

THE BRIEFING

Frequently, the most effective demonstration of public relations in action lies in the briefing before any action is taken.

This is a fundamental example of the initiative public relations must demonstrate. Rare is the year or the company so motionless that there will be cause for concern only a few times over an impending development or explosive situation. The alert public relations man will sense these situations before they're in full bloom and, in view of the serious implications they hold for the company, will marshal a defense. His biggest function is first to identify the trouble; then, in proportion to the problem, create an internal management review. The pros and cons of action—or no action—should be made while the options are open to the company; decisions made as to what internal and external postures the company should adopt and, conceivably, what corrective measures should be launched immediately.

Typical of developments that would warrant just such a briefing are these: prospects for a hot summer in a core city in which the company has a major plant operation, growing community irritation over dirt and noise stemming from construction activity, same for air pollution, union agitation in the plant, pending automation of phases of the manufacturing process.

Realistically, public relations in some corporations may be reluctant, or may not be empowered, to call a summit meeting on its own say so. That does not minimize its responsibility. It still can take up the problem with the chief executive and, if it is presented cogently and compellingly, management itself will no doubt follow through and call for a full-dress briefing.

CAN IT BE MEASURED

If the way could be found to measure public relations performance against results per dollar spent, the millennium would have arrived—not alone for public relations practitioners, but for kindred spirits in other creative pursuits— advertising, for one. But as their counterparts in advertising invest enormously—and perhaps a bit self-consciously—in Neilsen reports and motivational studies, and frenetically probe the id and ego of the consumer to try to learn what makes him tick, public relations practitioners are no less conscientious in their search for the key to security. For certainly, if they can prove that public relations pays off, in specifics, not in sanctimonious abstractions, then *hallelujah,* here comes the annuity!

For management, possibly bedazzled by promises of computerized analyses, or overwhelmed by test samples, surveys and any number of imaginative approaches to solve this vexing problem, the only practical counsel is: do not look for or anticipate concrete evidence of results, and do not be disappointed with the sparsity of it. This will inevitably come, but first we must develop a more scientific blueprint of what really motivates people to the degree that we can positively predict their reactions (which is beyond our capabilities today). Meanwhile, public relations is no less precise on the subject than are the sociologists and other behavioral scientists.

174

Because public relations has for too long been largely intuitive, it perhaps has the most pressing need for more scientific inputs, for incorporating more orderliness and precision in its modus operandi. However lean the body of knowledge is in understanding people's reactions, attitudes and opinions, public relations has an obligation to use the best of it, and to apply it to its myriad activities to get some measure of impact—even if it isn't conclusive. Management, for its part, should encourage such effort and not bewail the paucity of irrefutable results.

Despite these scientific drawbacks, there is no shortage of ingenious ideas and well-intentioned and imaginative efforts to harness the technology of our age in order to impart at least a pseudo-scientific air to public relations programming. Let us look at some of the currently favored techniques along these lines.

Most impressive, superficially, are those systems for measurement built around electronic computers. One such technique, sold commercially as a service by PR Data, Inc., offers to provide a quantitative analysis of publicity operations. A pioneering application, developed to full bloom in collaboration with a client, Mutual of New York (MONY), offers a means of controlling the flow of specific messages directed to a variety of external publics important to MONY. Output is later related to input; in other words, the level of efficiency of the material generated by the public relations staff in documented. The method is called Public Relations Electronic Planning and Review (PREPAR). Essentially, in MONY's case, it set specific priorities for the company's editorial campaign and evaluated results received, i.e., newspaper clippings, against those benchmarks. The objectives set were legitimate and attainable: to emphasize the corporate growth of MONY, stress its financial soundness and personnel development activity, and also its good corporate citizenship. Each point—called a message—was given a priority ranking. Each story had to bring in two of the four points originally set for editorial priority.

Each release produced by MONY's public relations staff was coded for punched-card use, indicating the story number, the publicity number, the messages "loaded in," the date and the publication. The computer readout report, based on returns, covers a variety of factors: the number of messages per story printed, the number of stories written vs the number of stories printed, the total inches of newsspace obtained, and the cumulative circulation of the editorial coverage represented. Further, each story is given a "value index" which is a quality reading placed on the story reflecting its competitive position in the paper. A page-one item obviously gets a higher value index number than a story buried in the classified ads.

The over-all report is impressive. For a one-year period the MONY boxscore showed that one story appeared in print for every three written; that 53 per cent of the stories had three or more messages important to MONY; that they averaged 1.51 messages per story printed; and that insurance trade and business publications showed a 65 per cent pickup of releases sent them by MONY; daily and weekly newspapers, a 29 per cent usage.

But, this is seductive, because the analysis is perhaps as misleading as it is informative. It does not demonstrate anything new *in measuring* public relations activity.

A more expansive use of PREPAR has been made by The Goodyear Tire & Rubber Company. For the first quarter of '68, Goodyear and PR Data, Inc. developed a three-way computerized analysis of publicity activity. One, was an analysis of corporate publicity, the second was a comprehensive computer study of marketing and product publicity for eight divisions, and the third study was an electronic analysis of the extent, range and scope of Goodyear publicity versus that of its three major competitors.

The corporate analysis indicated, for example, that 77.5

per cent of publicity generated was in Goodyear's key market areas and key trade and business-financial publications (as planned), and that the program balanced out with 43 per cent of the effort directed toward such corporate goals as growth, financial stability, research, management depth and citizenship, and 57 per cent in support of marketing objectives, i.e., product publicity, etc.

The company's showing *vis-à-vis* their traditional competitors, Firestone, Goodrich and Uniroyal (as measured in 65 control cities), showed Goodyear recording the heaviest publicity: 89 per cent, compared to 5.5% for Firestone, 3% for Goodrich and 2.5% for Uniroyal. But it also indicated that, while Goodyear emphasized marketing and product publicity support, its competitors directed the major share of their efforts to general corporate publicity; Firestone achieving, for example, an identity of 73 per cent, as compared to Goodyear's 43 per cent in this area.

Public relations vice president Robert H. Lane, of Goodyear, is not surprised by this, since his program, by design, puts considerable weight on what he calls the "meat and potato" aspects, or marketing support. This is, of course, subject to change, IF the competitive reading should suggest a new strategy. Lane readily acknowledges that studies themselves are a statistical measure, or a quantitative one, largely —not qualitative. Still, he thinks it's the beginning of a breakthrough in learning how to harness the electronic brain to serve the public relations profession. Certainly, he says, it introduces some orderliness to his own operation, which in itself, begets the discipline necessary not only to get things done, but to get the right things done.

Despite its space-age showmanship, the system merely substitutes electronic muscle for human labor to analyze clippings, add volume, tally circulation, "read out" geographic coverage, and aid in working out an array of percentages that give an impression of scientific communications planning. In those ways it is, perhaps, more efficient, but it does not constitute a major step in measuring results. One severe limitation lies in its raw material; it measures publicity copy only (and I trust we've made the point many times earlier that public relations has more arrows to its bow than a press release).

Too it makes, understandably, some arbitrary judgments. The so-called "value index" is an obvious one. This gives the relative measure of one story to another by such factors as length, location, etc. But it does not—because it cannot—measure impact. In fact, it cannot pin down whether or not the story was actually read at all. Some questions, too, must be raised over the technique of weighing space value. This is calculated by cost per thousand, meaning that management paid, for instance, 16.4¢ per thousand for stories accumulating 191.6 million total circulation. This is sophistry; circulation measurement is a viable instrument only when complete control over the message and the media (in terms of when and where published) is implicit. Stories that hinge on a third party's judgment (the editor's) of the news content cannot be measured against such an inflexible benchmark. Furthermore, this presupposes that editorial and advertising space are of equal impact—a fact that not even the most ardent advertising manager would support. Besides, this has always been a fruitless debate.

However, PREPAR—as an effort to train a staff to write news stories with more purpose than puffery, and to channel these stories to the proper publications—can play a distinct role in introducing organization and efficiency. The very fact that it facilitates the analyzing procedures adds a dimension accepted in principle but not always employed in public relations procedures. It is a provocative hint of what may some day be, but it still does not solve the perennial problem of measurement of results.

Another attempt to bend computers to public relations also came up with an electronic short circuit. Hill & Knowlton, one of the nation's larger public relations counseling firms, harnessed computers to provide another type of qualitative measurement. Basically, they've used computers for relating the types of audiences reached to specific client objectives. To this end, they developed an "audience profile chart" which, as the name implies, furnished a breakdown of the composition of the publics targeted for various clients. Thus, they're able not only to electronically count clippings and compute coverage, but, also, to relate such coverage by audience to the objectives of the client. For example, circulation of publicity on behalf of a client like the American Iron & Steel Institute is more than numbers if it is directed to architects, engineers, contractors and builders; this is the sort of analysis the computers plus the audience profile chart can provide.

Such analysis enables them to spot soft areas (looking to editorial coverage) and to beef-up publicity aimed at such areas. Or, more important, it may detect a poor mix of audiences; the publicity is being generated but not in the right places. Thus a reorientation is instituted.

Again, the computer adds only the assets of its electronic capability to systems and procedures that can be, and often are, being accomplished by other means. It has, of course, the value of speed, efficiency and the intangible extra imparted by the sophistication of the approach.

Buoyed by this mastery of computers, Hill & Knowlton took another tack to increase the utilization of computers. Working with computer programming experts, they attempted to computerize the creative aspects of public relations. Specifically, the idea was to evaluate the language and psychological appeal of actual public relations material. The first step was to create a "model public." Once constructed, its profile was fed into the computer. Then several hundred thousand words, gleaned from releases, booklets, etc., written on behalf of a client interested in this public, were also fed into the computer. The words fed in were compared, electronically, with the words already stored that represented the model. Ideally, the computer was to indicate the impact of communication on the model public by electronically appraising the two sets of words.

As former chairman John Mapes ruefully admits, what the computer said wasn't too usable. The results were neither clear enough nor crisp enough to be of practical value.

But it can be anticipated that greater sophistication in learning how to talk to a computer will improve this kind of dialogue. Moreover, it is another indication of bold experimentation.

The real problem of applying computers to public relations is not a problem of the machine, but of the man, in the opinion of one who professionally straddles both sides of the issue. Robert G. Strayton, director of public relations and merchandising for Honeywell's Electronic Data Processing division, points out that even the most casual request for computer-based data generally creates a mountain of statistics, research, demographics and other facts to be sorted, classified, formatted, transcribed, stored, read, analyzed, re-stored, re-formatted, printed out and delivered. At this point the public relations executive has to make the final decision. The entire process is only as worthwhile to the executive as the data he started with.

Strayton points out that in his view it will be decades before we are able to capture the types of data in which high confidence can be placed in making public relations decisions. Short of the decision-making process, though, he feels that there are several areas where computers can be put to work effectively: to develop a balance of external communication tools, to develop feedback on reactions to campaigns, and as a production tool in communication, by maintaining mailing lists, producing letters, etc.*

* The widespread interest in the use of computers in public relations, together with the misinformation spread concerning such application, prompted us to ask Mr. Strayton to elaborate on the subject. He did. It's in the Appendix. It's the first "White Paper" on the subject.

180

In the interim, public relations will find it more beneficial to rely on more pedestrian procedures of measurement. There is no shortage of reliable and legitimate organizations to set programs, literally to fit any corporate pocketbook, to help gauge the reactions to public relations efforts. Just so long as you don't expect such surveys to come up with positive measurements, they are of incalculable value.

The Gallup organization's Public Relations Index is just such a plan. The basic fee for one general population profile a year is $5,000 and this covers a door-to-door sampling of some 1,500 people. It draws upon the 400 or so Gallup interviewers who are constantly out in the field.

What do you get for this? For one thing, a chance to identify a public relations problem or areas where the reputation or regard for the corporation can be improved— or, a chance simply to verify the magnitude of a problem already known or suspected to exist. The general study, tailored to the company, would cover the gamut—by sex, age groups, religion, businessmen, financial areas, etc.—in sampling attitudes and opinions. It would tell the company what the public thinks of it on every key phase of its activity. A single survey is, of course, like standing on one leg; it automatically requires a follow-up poll to provide some indication of whether or not the situation has improved. If it has, public relations will be gratified, but if the results are the same as before or worse, public relations will remind you of how difficult it is to change opinions. They'll be right in both instances, and this is the fundamental weakness in such surveys: they're an indication but not an infallible one.

Without question, however, the public relations program that makes periodic use of independent surveys will be a better one, if for no other reason than the attempt at self-criticism represented in this honest effort to get some feedback on its activities.

CHAPTER ELEVEN

The Folklore of Public Relations—
(Myths That Muddy Its Image)

The public relations profession has long needed generous doses of the same medicine its practitioners regularly prescribe for their managements. Until recently it's been a case of, "do as I say, not as I do." But the sleeping giant stirs itself and has begun to counterattack against those who characterize its daily bread as "high hokum," or deprecate its talents as "Dale Carnegie writ large," and "Big Brotherly skills at brainwashing." The Public Relations Society of America's accreditation program is inexorably moving to put teeth in its program for higher professional and moral standards. Its Code of Ethics for PRSA members may be irrelevant for nonmembers but it's at least a subliminal deterrent, if not a brake.

But, can public relations for public relations really succeed in coping with the basic misunderstandings of their profession—a picture not made any clearer by use of such slick portrayals as "invisible sell," "velvet hammer," or "black art"?

Nor are prospects for a calm, reasoned view of public relations greatly enhanced by popularity of such parlor games as "the Propaganda Game." Although its introduction is careful to make the point that propaganda—publicity to most of us—is a noble art as well as a sometimes nefarious one, the ground rules of the game take a decided Machiavel-

182

lian turn. Consider the techniques basic to playing it. There are the techniques of self-deception, the techniques of language, the techniques of irrelevance, the techniques of exploitation, the techniques of maneuver, plus an ingenious array of "red-herring" dodges: non sequiturs, faulty analogies, diversion, hasty generalizations, attacking a straw man and victory by definition.

It is a paradox of our time—a cybernetic era of information explosions and communications revolutions—that public relations, in spite of this almost perfect environment for growth and understanding, finds itself facing an "understanding gap." This gap is not confined to what public relations is or where it is going. It also relates to where it is going and how.

This may seem far-fetched, especially in view of the fact that for a profession or trade that's grown, acorn to oak, into a business billing in excess of $2 billion, it seems to be in vigorous health. However, it is a communications axiom that what other people don't know about you can hurt you, but what they don't understand about you can destroy you.

Thanks to a more or less spontaneous folklore of disparagement, public relations is still a murky business. Whether or not its own medicine can cope with its illness, which is more of a 24-hour bug than a malignancy, depends to a large degree not on the diagnosis, but instead, on the attitude of the patient. Simply speaking, it's: "Physician heal thyself." If public relations people are candid and objective about their own shortcomings, caused more by default than by commission, then cure is possible. Those in the profession must bear the burden for permitting a mythology to build up which no more fills in the picture than Chinese food does the appetite. The family of myths that have been perpetrated grew to prominence primarily because they were never effectively challenged by those who had the credentials and facts to do so. Public relations people have either been too busy, too inarticulate, or too complacent, or have just lacked the commitment to speak up.

So management, very much as a consequence of this unclear path, is either too timorous to venture into the never-never land of psychedelic communication, or plunges in with firm resolve to keep a close rein on publicity—to hold it in its place. For despite the pyramiding effect of the success of public relations activity on business in general, many, embracing it for the first time as a formal management activity, are hard pressed to understand the nature of their own creation. It is hardly satisfying or edifying to say simply that it is what you make of it: press agent or communications pundit, reporter of corporate minutiae, or public affairs strategist.

Nor is the solution to put the burden of interpretation and translation upon management. Public relations people, from the junior staff writer to the Brahmans of the profession, could perhaps use some autopsychoanalysis. If they would re-examine some of the shibboleths they persist in citing, and if they would learn to curb their enthusiasm, the understanding gap would be appreciably narrowed. It should go without reminder that the esoteric jargon that tries to translate public relations activity in such terms as blurb, ink, handout, split page, peg, plugs and flimsies has no place in the lexicon of the corporate public relations man—certainly not in management councils.

While this book is directed to management, perhaps some candid self-analysis of the professional faults will contribute more to understanding this business than all the words dispensed earlier. It is true that sometimes you learn quicker what something is by finding out what it is not. This may sound like sophistry, but it is as good a rationale as any to apply here.

One of the biggest areas of misunderstanding, within and without the business, concerns the priority generally given to newspaper skills as basic for apprenticeship. This is like say-

184

ing that a good memory makes a quarterback. As was pointed out earlier in this book, the ability to write lucidly, quickly and with a certain amount of freshness is of course indispensable for the public relations man or woman who wants to get involved. All public relations activity must at one time or another deal with communication. The transmission of ideas, philosophies and concepts inevitably involves the written word. Newspaper training, or its equivalent, should be held in high regard largely because it teaches the disciplines of reporting—objectivity, clarity and speed. *But,* and few of the pros bring this out, the ability to decide *what* to write and *when* to write and *if* to write is an even more significant requirement. This judgment is not necessarily a legacy of newspaper training. It springs from a broader background. It is a by-product not only of education but of sophistication. To be tuned in on the world in which we live suggests a background of interests and experiences richer and more diversified than most newspaper training alone. That is why the newspaper route is no longer the "yellow brick road" to public relations entry that it once was.

Speaking of writing, computers have tried to intrude here, too. A computer wrote 800 news stories on the 1,500 June graduates at the University of Detroit. It took but 12 minutes (and another 50 hours to program the electronic "brain"), zipping off the stories in teletype form, sorted according to zip-code numbers, for newspapers in 42 states and 23 foreign countries. But writers are not about to be automated out of existence. The *Wall Street Journal* reports that the University public relations people had to make 25 long-distance calls to correct major errors.

Moving into the mythology more deeply, you stumble first over the hallowed Myth of the Mimeograph Machine, or the notion that's been allowed to spring up weedlike that all problems are equally susceptible to amelioration by press release. Small wonder that some critics believe that public relations doesn't have much more dimension than this, that

185

its results are more quantitative than qualitative. It is true that those engaged in it are preoccupied with techniques and mechanics. These are measures of activity and they hope, tangibles that will contribute to personal economic gain. And since early public relations people almost universally came from newspapers or magazines, it logically followed that a story—press release if you prefer—is one technique they are most dependent on and familiar with.

Public relations, of course, has made more progress than perfecting its propaganda machine; it certainly has made more tangible contributions than is revealed by publicity, or the resulting clippings. Take just one area, that of exploring the relationship of the enterprise to its social responsibilities.

Virtue is still pale news next to sin, so business' and industry's positive accomplishments are buried deep in the newspaper. But company after company, industry upon industry, is taking a more active role today in politics, in civic affairs, in the wars against poverty, against pollution, against narcotics. And it is working to improve relations with government, with its community, and with academic circles, including students.

Apropos of this, public affairs activity—a sort of mutation of the public relations that spawned it—is the fastest-growing segment of American business. Ten years ago only a handful of companies had anything resembling a public affairs program. Today there are, at the minimum, over 500 such corporate programs.

MYTH OF PUBLICS

Closely related is the *Myth of Publics,* a principal deity. This myth says that multitudes of people are easily divisible into groups, cultures and sub-cultures. This has a nice anthropological ring to it, but, unfortunately, you can't break down 200 million Americans into neat packages of publics— the employee public, the stockholder public, the financial public, etc. You can't ascribe to these sub-cultures uniform characteristics that will be responsive to, and motivated by, a basic pattern of messages concocted by public relations. This myth is refined by endorsement of a co-myth, the *Myth of the Lists,* a compartmentalization technique that stems from the same kind of antediluvian thinking. It concludes, for example, that once cultural similarities of employees, stock- holders or the community are identified they are relatively homogeneous in their interests and can be appealed to through the same communication. Then public relations pro- ceeds on the somewhat naïve belief that it makes friends by explaining things to people. So, the more you cram people with information about your company, *voilà,* the better they'll like you!

In this context "publics" is a myth. You needn't be a sociologist to recognize that leaders have different motivations from those of the public at large; no successful insurance salesman would use the same pitch on all of his prospects. Yet, day in and day out, public relations repeats this decisive tactical error. Why? Part of the answer lies in the resolute homage to the goddess of the clipping books, as though communication can be weighed by the pound. Saturation publicity is tangible evidence of our hard work, so we credit it with virtues it hasn't earned and never will.

The hard fact is that there is no substitute for the careful, more precise cultivation of, or communication with, key individuals who are the catalysts for action in any group— politics, the community, customers, and employees.

The head of a Pittsburgh fund-raising firm has ob- served that, after 5,300 campaigns, even in a very large community the real decision-makers never exceed more than 40 or 50. It is astonishing to discover how regularly decisions as to what a community or its organizations shall do come from agreements made among a half-dozen or a dozen people.

MYTH OF CONSENSUS

An especially dangerous trap is the *Myth of Consensus*. It's a sort of theory that the public relations man has to be nice to everyone (no doubt, so they will reciprocate), and has to head off possible bad opinions of company action by preaching caution, temporization or expediency.

Under these ground rules the entrepreneurial spirit of this country would have been aborted early in the 18th century. Henry Ford would have gone broke painting his Tin Lizzies every color of the rainbow to suit individual tastes; the aversion to dissent would have short-circuited the growth of aviation, and the cornucopia of new products (that please some and irritate others) would have been a hollow horn. The public relations man who is too timid to say "no" at appropriate times, or fails to recognize that not *every* corporate action can be a popular one, is isolated from reality, and of little value to himself or to his company.

MYTH OF PRETENSES

This brings us to an interesting home-brewed myth, the *Myth of Pretenses*. It's true that public relations has achieved a degree of corporate status. Whether this citizenship is real or counterfeit depends more upon public relations' future actions than on its past history. Public relations must not pretend to know all the answers, or even the questions. To an extent perhaps unequaled in the history of its profession, conscientious self-examination is denying it that comfort. The rapid pace of social change and the instability of values stemming from geographical and social mobility demand a new responsiveness and broader, more comprehensive service than can ever be rendered by the mimeograph machine alone. It can't be business-as-usual.

EXTRAVAGANT GOALS

Part of public relations' problem in communicating its role stems from its penchant for insisting upon immediate all-out action, or setting extravagant goals, as if to set out to achieve anything else suggests a lack of sincerity or capability, or confidence. I call it the *Myth of the Golden Goal*. Too often, public relations directors want to change everything, to do it all at once. Actually, they change little, save possibly that they diminish somewhat the credibility of their claims of achievements, which never, somehow, come to pass. If public relations people resist the temptation to be overly ambitious, there is every likelihood that, once free of this bind, they will be able to make a number of important incremental advances.

In his zeal to be a combination Disraeli and Nostradamus the public relations man often forgets that he still can only advise. Maybe it will afford his some solace to remember, as the saying goes, that one can give advice but not the wisdom to profit from it.

His fundamental role is to be a catalyst, to bring creativity to bear upon problems. He must have the sensitivity, curiosity and imagination to anticipate a situation before it grows into a problem, and later into a crisis.

Public relations must be capable of convincing management of the possibilities of danger, of the need to change. Here is where public relations cashes in on what credibility it has stored up. The status of its bank account will be a direct reflection of the professionalism it brings to the situation.

MYTH OF THE ACADEMICIAN

A popular thesis these days is that of emphasizing the need for generalists in public relations, for a greater infusion of social science oriented people, of the need for a grounding in political science, in economics, in sociology, even anthropology and psychology. In time, this concept, which implies that an academician is the ideal public relations candidate, may become the most troublesome myth of all. No business is more vulnerable to untested theory or more often tempted by it than public relations. This is not only an action-centered business, but it is a pragmatic, realistic business, no more hospitable to naïveté than is engineering or sales or manufacturing.

This is not to say public relations can't improve its intellectual level, but theoreticians or pure intellectuals will find its kind of firing-line activity uncomfortable, at best. Actually, education is really a concept. The main fact about it is that there is no such thing, per se. Chesterton points out that education is like transmission. It is not an object, but a method.

For those in public relations, education, in this context, doesn't mean textbook familiarity with the jargon of sociology, or of psychology. Instead it means some honest concern for and research into why people react the way they do to various stimuli. It means the kind of intuitive awareness that comes from broad experience with mob psychology, with sticky labor situations. It means more than a surface acquaintance with the question of the survival of private education, and with the problem of urban development, or with the dilemmas facing a nation trying to cope with the problem of 34 million Americans trapped in prisons of bleak poverty.

We've all read about our collegians' alleged disenchantment with business. Well, many of these troubled critics— even some of the young radicals and self-proclaimed student nihilists—will, in time, become the activists of business and industry. They will inevitably bring fresh style and emphasis to business. To establish any constructive rapport with these new business leaders, public relations in particular is going to have to demonstrate a new sophistication, too. It must be able to adjust to new ideas and new trends. The traditional organization and patterns of public relations behavior will just not be equal to the more extensive assignments expected of it in this period of change and growth. To put it another way, public relations must consciously condition itself to an attitude of "enlightened dissatisfaction," because if there's one thing certain about the way things are it is that they are uncertain; they will change—inevitably but surely.

And finally there is a sort of a tragic chicken-and-egg aspect to many public relations people's exaggerated humility. This leads us to the:

MYTH OF FALSE MODESTY

Management sometimes abuses public relations because it doesn't rate it that important; and those unfortunate public relations people acknowledging their low form of corporate citizenship are too self-conscious, hesitant or just afraid to boldly stand forth and earn the regard they yearn for. Whose fault is it? Which came first, the chicken or the egg? Regardless, public relations practitioners should stop worrying about the imagined transience of their positions and recognize the really pivotal role they do play. Consider only, if you will, the communications aspects. Business today exists in a nation that boasts some 10,000 newspapers, 8,000 magazines, 7,000 radio and television stations, publishes millions of books a year, broadcasts 1,500 hours of news a year, and puts some 7 million words on the wires to news media every day. Recognize once and for all the magnitude of the job, and the skill and judgment required, to edge your corporation

191

into this monsoon of information. Writing expert Dr. Rudolph Flesch, whose *Art of Readable Writing* was a notable milestone in de-gobbledygooking writing, says that after 20 years of observation he must report with dismay that business writing has deteriorated badly. Flesch, of whom Alan J. Gould, former executive editor of the Associated Press, said, "he has ideas that have played a major part in lifting writing habits out of some of their oldest ruts," refers to daily business correspondence as the bureaucratic language that's a product of modern civilization. Doesn't this inspire some confidence? You're a skilled communicator, probably the only one the corporation's got!

If the quarterback role played in this one area of communications isn't enough to build confidence, just read the daily paper carefully. Note corporate activity in ghetto reform; agonize if you will with the company heads undergoing a Washington committee grilling; note the criticism by consumer experts of producers of products familiar to all of us; picture the situation in the plant silent for the past few weeks because of a strike; puzzle out the motivations of the students picketing another plant, or why they're boycotting its goods; read of the multi-million-dollar gift of a corporation to a university; take some pride in new opportunities opened for hard-core unemployables by local business. And, when you're digesting all of this, bear one thing in mind: Someplace in the center of all of this diverse activity there is a public relations man. He's not setting policy, blowing whistles and giving orders, but he is sure to be in there with rolled-up sleeves making substantial contributions with intelligence, enthusiasm, sensitivity and professional expertise. He may not be indispensable, but things could be a lot different without him. Self-respect begins within.

Public Relations Counsel:
How to Choose and Why *

Management turns to public relations counsel principally for two reasons. One, it senses the need to broaden the perspective of its public relations conduct, but lacks the internal resources to objectively weigh what is needed and then know how to implement it. Two, management sees the need to get the job under way efficiently and professionally in considerably less time than the learning curve would permit if an in-house capability were to be developed. And, economics is very much a part of it. Despite the substantial fees customarily charged by the larger counseling firms—$25,000 to $65,000 annually—the range of professional services offered and geographic coverage provided would be exceedingly expensive for an individual company to underwrite.

The extent and manner of help provided by public relations consultants varies, of course, with individual situations. Fundamentally, public relations counseling is the professional service by specially trained and experienced persons helping management *diagnose* problems in the public relations area, recommending solutions to these problems, and then helping to match action to counsel by undertaking to execute the necessary programs. Although today, more and

* Based on a statement from the Counsellor's Section of the Public Relations Society of America.

193

more, the counseling firms are activists, plunging heavily into program implementation, a sizable number, including some of the more respected public relations counselors, do largely just that—counsel.

Whether the counselor plays a limited role or is fully involved in the activity of a program, he is action-oriented in that his thinking is directed toward improved managerial performance. The public relations counselor's most important function inevitably is that of urging and persuading management toward sound courses of action.

A condensed list of areas in which the public relations consultant may be of service to business would include:

Establishment and definition of short-range or long-range public relations goals.

Counsel and guidance to management on actions or policies which affect public relations goals.

Support of the marketing program, including product or process publicity—news releases, feature articles, case studies, audio visual aids, press, radio and television coverage.

Stockholder and financial relations—annual, quarterly or interim reports to shareholders, special releases to financial news media, assistance with the annual meeting, liaison with security analysts, investment dealers, and the professional investment community.

Employee and internal communications—company publications, information program for employees on profits, the economics of industry, quality control, and over-all company operations.

Community relations—counsel on public relations policies at the local plant or branch office level, liaison with local news media, assistance in establishing policies of corporate giving, staging special events such as "open houses" and plant tours.

Government relations—international, federal, state and local—public relations counseling and liaison with agencies

194

or officials whose policies influence the operations of the client.

Evaluations and measurement—analysis of the effectiveness of public relations programs, application and use of budget, and attainment of identifiable objectives.

CHARACTERISTICS OF PUBLIC RELATIONS COUNSELING FIRMS

A public relations consulting firm normally comprises a group of experienced professionals skilled in the techniques of research, analysis, communication and the social sciences. Such firms are equipped, through the experience and training of their principals and seasoned staff personnel, to understand the specific as well as the immediate and long-range requirements of clients. Newspapers and such other communications media as magazines and radio were early sources of personnel to the counseling profession, so professional writing skill is a common denominator. These sources continue to feed talent to the profession, although the greater depth and variety of public relations services now required for competence in counseling have been drawing an increasing number of professionals into practice from other areas—personnel, law, education, marketing, finance and psychology.

Higher education contributes an increasing share of the talent now entering the profession. At least 170 colleges and universities offer public relations courses or degrees. Some 350 teachers or professors of public relations, nationwide, have been identified, which gives some measure of its popularity, not necessarily of its competence.

The mushrooming of counseling firms—there are well over 1,500 consultant firms and individual counselors, and some 500 are represented in the Counselor's Section of the Public Relations Society of America alone—has inevitably

195

spawned a growing number of specialists. Today there are firms dealing principally in financial relations, product publicity, trade association work and service for government agencies or governments themselves. There are public relations firms specializing in education, in municipal services, in health and welfare, in the arts and in virtually every other identifiable field.

HOW A PUBLIC RELATIONS CONSULTANT WORKS

There is only one sound premise on which to base an effective relationship with a public relations consultant. And that is that public relations *is* a top management function. The successful client-consultant relationship stems from that premise which, after all, reflects no different understanding from that which is involved in working with management consultants, per se.

The public relations consultant counsels the chief executive or other members of management on basic public relations problems of the enterprise. Management (to get a practical return on the dollars invested) must provide effective backing for the consultant's work, respect the fact that he is an independent party, and keep in close touch with, and coordinate, if necessary, the activity resulting. Management often will find it necessary to prepare the organization for change—change suggested by the consultant for just and due cause.

This reciprocal responsibility of both client, and consultant to take appropriate action on recommendations is a cardinal rule. It is one of the most obvious and the one most violated. Management often walks away from this responsibility, assuming homage to the subject duly paid by simply retaining the "brains" to do the job. Some public relations consultants, finding strong resistance to change and the lack of real belief in the need for any, capitulate too easily and do "it the way management wants it."

By and large, though, the public relations consultant will begin his work for a client by appraising the public relations problems and potentials. Or he may conduct his own research to determine the validity of those problems management is alleged to have. Either step requires close liaison between client and counsel and is based on full, unrestricted disclosures of management's needs, goals, and such problems or obstacles as exist.

Preliminary analysis may reveal a requirement for further, more professional research. Public relations (or management, for that matter) may sense, but not actually be able to document, what attitudes the various publics important to the company hold toward it. Too much is at stake to rely principally on intuition. Research to determine these facts and others more scientifically is often a primary function of the public relations counselor. In some instances the magnitude of the job is such that he will recommend engaging outside specialists in opinion research, attitude analysis, etc. However it's done, it's all part and parcel of the vital fact-finding task that should precede any formal development of a public relations program.

Following such research, the consultant presents a clearly developed program for action. It will be keyed to the client's specific requirements and will reflect analysis of the results of the attitude studies, and an interpretation of what the findings mean in terms of actions and activities designed for achieving corporate objectives.

If company management is clear on what its objectives are, the consultant's program will attest to the validity of these objectives and recommend a realistic timetable for achieving them. Ethical counsel will never predict instant miracles; a year's program generally can measure up to the ambition of substantial progress, but total success is as rare as 100% achievement is in any program.

197

On the other hand, corporate management may be quite vague as to what it expects from public relations, except in very fuzzy and general terms. In such instances, the consultant will suggest objectives, these being oriented to the fundamental corporate objectives of the company itself.

The program of action will be specific. It will outline the reasoning for recommended action, the methods to be followed, the techniques to be employed, the timetable or scheduling of activity, and what results may reasonably be anticipated (but never guaranteed).

All of this will be presented in formal review for management's endorsement before proceeding. Accompanying the program will, of course, be a detailed budget analysis.

The decision to proceed and the basic responsibility for the scope of the activity belong to management. It is not obligated to accept the program in toto; alternatives to various activities may be suggested, others deleted for a variety of reasons, including policy. But it should be borne in mind that while the ultimate success of the public relations effort requires unanimity of agreement on fundamental objectives, the public relations adviser has the greater competence to judge the appropriateness of the action plan. Excessive doctoring of this portion of the campaign by management will not only seriously weaken the total effort, but it begins to undermine the endeavor by weakening the essential nature of the relationship between consultant and client—a relationship that must be based on mutual understanding and confidence. In the final analysis, the consultant can only *assist* in the solution of management's problems; he is likely to do this in proportion to his ability and to the degree of cooperation he receives.

For all of the advanced planning and careful scheduling, public relations cannot be locked into an inflexible formula. It must be able to respond quickly to change. After all, it is dealing with the most volatile of all ingredients—people's constantly changing opinions and attitudes—and in an environment where the ground rules may change swiftly, through economic, political or social events.

A written contract may be employed, although some of the most effective client-counsel relationships have existed for years without formalized agreements.

RELATIONSHIP TO CLIENT'S OWN PUBLIC RELATIONS DEPARTMENT

Public relations counselors are often retained by companies with sizable public relations departments of their own. In such cases the use of outside counsel obviously supplements the internal department, and the total effectiveness of the over-all public relations program is enhanced.

Companies with internal departments may seek outside aid for five reasons: (1) to provide extra help for special projects requiring an above-normal level of public relations activity, (2) to obtain counsel on a long-term planning basis, (3) to add dimension to the public relations effort beyond the capabilities or manpower of the existing staff, (4) to audit the existing public relations capability and make recommendations for strengthening it, or, (5) to help a client establish an internal organization where none exists.

A client having its own public relations department obtains many additional advantages when outside counsel is retained. One benefit is perspective. The client's public relations department may, of necessity, have experience limited to the client's specific markets and products. Another benefit is the wider range of skills, talent, experience, and specialized ability that public relations counsel can bring to bear on a management problem. In most cases, these go beyond what is available within a company. Broad experience that a public relations counsel accumulates serving many clients is richly productive when applied to an individual organization.

Outside, independent counsel brings a fresh viewpoint

to the over-all public relations program on a continuing basis. Although equally dedicated to the best interests of the client, outside counsel is freer to ask challenging questions of management, to examine past and present policies with professional, impartial perspective. Above all, the public relations counseling firm will offer a breadth and depth of professional experience and sound judgment not available elsewhere.

Some companies find it expedient to direct an existing internal organization to concentrate on all internal public relations activities, while retaining counsel for the external activities. If there is a close rapport between the two, this can work out very successfully, resulting in a comprehensive and diversified program.

The obvious areas of activity that might tax the resources of an internal group are projects like major anniversary celebrations, a major new product introduction or a special community or city-wide campaign. Recently, the need for professional guidance on such priority topics as financial and investor relations, urban relations and labor relations have generated corporate assignments for consultants, the management rationale being that these are somewhat beyond the scope and conventional inventory of the responsibilities of the existing public relations department.

SELECTING PUBLIC RELATIONS COUNSEL

Ideally, the organization seeking public relations counsel will be clear on what it wants and what it expects to accomplish through retention of public relations counsel. As a practical matter, its surface objectives may be only a facade to cover an intuitive feeling that more planning and performance should be given this relatively new area of management responsibility. Whether management's needs are strongly fixed or superficial, the same basic questions should be asked in inquiry of any counseling organization. For example:

What is the professional competence and background of the principals of the firm?

How much experience has been in fields of particular importance to us?

What is the general reputation of the firm? Has it a reputation for integrity and professional standing?

Who are the present clients? How long have they been served by this organization? What is the rate of client turnover?

Who among the principals and staff of the counseling firm will be working on our account? What are their qualifications, special training and background, as related to our needs?

Most reputable public relations counseling firms will not engage in speculative presentations. They are retained for their capacity to provide services based on their problem-solving ability and their aptitude to provide a creative resource for management.

HOW PUBLIC RELATIONS FIRMS CHARGE FOR THEIR SERVICES

Most client-counsel relationships start with an acknowledged need for public relations assistance, and the question of cost is related to the extent of the work to be undertaken, the time involved, and the number of staff personnel required.

There is no rule of thumb, no yardstick to be applied to establish rigid budgetary formulas. Professional public relations counseling firms, however, are prepared to give you an accurate estimate of the costs involved, after they have determined your needs, through conferences or a preliminary analysis. (*Text continued on page 213*)

Reporting Required for	Securities and Exchange Commission	New York Stock Exchange
Accounting— Change in Methods or Change in Fiscal Year	8-K * may be required if change in method results in or is related to a material revaluation of assets or restatement of capital share account.	Notice to Exchange if change in method is substantial. 8-K if filed. Must disclose effect of any change in next succeeding interim and annual report.
Acquisition or Merger	8-K if company or majority-owned subsidiary acquires a significant (15 per cent increase in total assets or revenues) amount of assets or business other than in course of business or if registrant issues more than 5 per cent of additional securities. Proxy soliciting material or Registration Statement may also be required.	8-K if filed. No other formal notice required.
Amendment of Charter or Bylaws	8-K if matter subject to stockholders' approval or if change materially modifies rights of holders of any class of registered securities.	Four copies of material sent to stockholders in respect to proposed changes. Certified copies of changes when effective. 8-K required for amendments to charter or by-laws.

* Generally speaking, Form 8-K must be filed within 10 days after the close of each month during which an event occurs which must be reported on this form. There are exceptions, which should be discussed with counsel.

† Items which, in our opinion, are clearly timely disclosure matters have been marked TD. The NYSE "timely disclosure provisions" require issuance of a press release on "immediate release" basis to "one or more of the newspapers of general circulation in New York City which regularly publish financial news and simultaneously to Dow Jones & Company, Inc. and one or more of the other major national news services"—AP, UPI,

REPORTING REQUIREMENTS

American Stock Exchange	Midwest and Pacific Stock Exchange	Generally Recommended Publicity Practice— All Companies
8-K if filed. Same as NYSE.	8-K if filed. Notice of any material change.	Ordinarily no publicity at time of change. Recommended effort in subsequent financial reports to relate old and new financial methods/old and new reporting periods.
8-K if filed. Same as NYSE.	8-K if filed. Timely disclosure provisions apply.	TD: † Recommend publicity immediately following directors' action. Earlier comment may be required by unusual market action or by rumors circulating about event.
8-K. Same as NYSE.	8-K. Certified copy and opinion of counsel, three copies of mailings to stockholders.	Recommend publicity if change alters rights or interests of shareholders.

Reuters. The Exchange manual also states, "When news of a material event which may affect the value of a company's securities or influence investment decisions is released shortly before the opening or during market hours . . . it is recommended that the Department of Stock List of the Exchange be notified by telephone no later than simultaneously with the announcement of the event to the news media." The manual then warns that the Exchange may temporarily halt trading until, normally, "15 minutes after appearance of the news on the Dow-Jones news ticker."

(Reprinted from *Public Relations Journal* by permission, copyright April, 1968. Table compiled by Robert W. Taft and Craig S. Thompson.)

Reporting Required for	Securities and Exchange Commission	New York Stock Exchange
Annual Report to Shareholders	Required by Section 13 of Securities Exchange Act of 1934 on Form 10-K to be filed no later than 120 days after close of fiscal year. Submit four copies of printed annual report with 10-K. Annual report must be delivered to shareholders with, or prior to, delivery of proxy material.	Published and submitted to shareholders at least 15 days before annual meeting but no later than three months after close of fiscal year. (See individual company listing agreement.) PROMPTEST POSSIBLE ISSUANCE URGED. Three copies to Exchange. Recommend release of audited figures as soon as available.
Disposition of Assets	8-K if company or majority owned subsidiary disposes of a significant amount of assets or business other than in normal course of business.	8-K if filed. In addition, prompt notice if disposition materially affects financial position of company or extent of its operations.
Dividends		Prompt notice to Exchange and IMMEDIATE publicity. Exchange requires telephone alert when the action is unusual (increase, decrease, omitting, etc.). Immediate means even while meeting is still in progress.
Form or Nature of Listed Securities Changed	8-K if constituent instruments defining rights have been materially modified or if rights are otherwise limited.	8-K if filed. At least 20 days prior notice of change in form or nature of securities or certificates.
Interim Earnings Statement	Form 9-K for first half of fiscal year only. Send to exchanges involved and to SEC within 45 days of close of period.	Quarterly. Publicity required—shareholder mailing recommended but not required. No set time limit but four to five weeks after close of period considered usual.

REPORTING REQUIREMENTS

American Stock Exchange	Midwest and Pacific Stock Exchange	Generally Recommended Publicity Practice— All Companies
10 days before meeting but no later than four months after close of fiscal year. PROMPTEST POSSIBLE ISSUANCE URGED. Three copies to Exchange. Recommend release of audited figures as soon as available.	MIDWEST: Mail with or prior to notice of annual meeting a report containing balance sheet, income statement, analysis of surplus account covering period since last report. Consolidated, certified copy to Exchange. PACIFIC: Copies to Exchange and shareholders 15 days before meeting, not more than 120 days after close of year.	TD: Publicity required. Recommend release of annual financial information as soon as available; second release at time printed report is issued.
8-K if filed. Same as NYSE.	8-K if filed. Same as NYSE.	TD: Immediate publicity, especially when assets consist of an entire product line, division, operating unit or a substantial part of the business.
Same as NYSE.	Publish promptly to shareholders any action. Notify Exchange.	TD: Publicity should be prepared in advance and released immediately on word of declaration. Publicity especially important when dividend rate changes.
8-K. Same as NYSE.	8-K. 10 day prior notice.	TD
Quarterly. Should be published within 45 days after end of fiscal quarter.	MIDWEST: Three copies to Exchange. PACIFIC: Semi-annual. Publish and submit four copies to Exchange.	TD

Reporting Required for	Securities and Exchange Commission	New York Stock Exchange
Listed Securities—Change in Rights or Privileges	8-K in event material modification or limitation —including restrictions on working capital or dividend payments.	8-K if filed. At least 20 day advance notice of proposed changes. May require change in listing agreement.
Listing on Another Exchange or Listing on an Exchange	Involved and extensive legal work is required.	(See Col. 1.)
Material Legal Proceedings	8-K at start and termination of material proceedings (see exceptions in 8-K item 3); any bankruptcy, receiverships, etc. or proceedings in which certain parties have interests adverse to company.	8-K sufficient unless proceeding bears on ownership, dividends, interest or principal of listed securities or to institution of receivership, bankruptcy, reorganization proceedings, etc.
Meetings of Stockholders	8-K required when security holders' vote required except as to procedural matters, selection of auditors or uncontested election of management nominees as listed in proxy statement.	8-K if filed. Prompt notice and publicity on significant occurrences. Also at least 10 days advance notice of record date or closing transfer books—plus four copies of proxy material.
Auditors Changed		Prompt notice of change in accounting firm which regularly audits company books.
Business Purposes Changed	8-K if registrant deems change of material of importance to security holders (consult counsel).	Prompt notice of any material change in general character or nature of business.
Capital Surplus Charges	8-K required for material restatement of capital share accounts.	Prior notice of any proposed substantial charge by company or by directly or indirectly controlled subsidiary.

REPORTING REQUIREMENTS

American Stock Exchange	Midwest and Pacific Stock Exchange	Generally Recommended Publicity Practice— All Companies
8-K if filed. Same as NYSE.	8-K if filed. 10 day prior notice. May require substitute listing application.	TD
(See Col. 1.)	(See Col. 1.)	Handled by exchange. Discuss with attorneys and public relations counsel well in advance.
8-K if filed. Same as NYSE.	8-K if filed.	Usually not, unless suit generates substantial negative or misleading publicity about company.
8-K if filed. Same as NYSE.	8-K if filed. MIDWEST: Three copies of proxy and notice to exchange. PACIFIC: Four copies of proxy material to Exchange.	Recommend inviting interested financial writers and advance preparation of news release.
Same as NYSE.		Normally no publicity —consider mention in annual report.
8-K if filed. Same as NYSE.	8-K if filed. PROMPT notice of any change in general character or nature of business.	TD: Recommend publicity where change may affect market for stock.
Same as NYSE.	8-K if filed.	Depends on circumstances.

Reporting Required for	Securities and Exchange Commission	New York Stock Exchange
Collateral Removed or Changed	8-K unless made pursuant to terms of an indenture qualified under Trust Indenture Act of 1939.	8-K. IMMEDIATE notice.
Conversion Rates— Changes in	8-K if material change.	Prompt publicity on any change in convertible security, or termination of conversion privilege when conversions have been occurring or appear imminent. Notice by mail to holders of record. Immediate notice to Exchange.
Decrease in Floating Supply of Stock	8-K if decreased more than 5 per cent of previously outstanding amount by payment of indebtedness or decreased more than 1 per cent by open market purchases.	Prompt notice when occasioned by actual or proposed deposit under voting trust agreements, etc., and brought to official attention of officers or directors.
Default upon Senior Securities	8-K if actual material default in principal, interest, sinking or purchase fund installment, etc., not cured within 30 days— and if indebtedness exceeds five per cent of total consolidated assets. 8-K if material arrearage in dividends not cured in 30 days for preferred registered or ranking securities.	8-K if filed. IMMEDIATE publicity and notification when and as soon as known.
Directors or Officers— Change in or Change of Control	8-K if change in control of corporation. New directors, officers or other insiders must personally file Form 3.	PROMPT notice of any change. 8-K if filed.

REPORTING REQUIREMENTS

American Stock Exchange	Midwest and Pacific Stock Exchange	Generally Recommended Publicity Practice— All Companies
8-K. Same as NYSE.	8-K.	Depends on indenture.
8-K if filed. Same as NYSE.	8-K if filed.	TD: Publicity should be timed to the event causing the change or termination of the conversion privilege. Immediate notice to statistical services.
Same as NYSE.	Same as NYSE.	Usually no publicity except that TD provisions may apply prior to purchase of own stock on open market.
8-K if filed. Same as NYSE.	8-K if filed. Publish promptly to holders. Notice to Exchange a reasonable time in advance.	TD
8-K if filed. Same as NYSE.	8-K if filed. Same as NYSE.	TD: Immediate announcement of any change in directors, officers or in control.

Reporting Required for	Securities and Exchange Commission	New York Stock Exchange
Proxy Material	Three preliminary copies at least 10 days prior to shareholder mailing. Eight finals not later than date sent to holders, plus three to each exchange where listed. If company does not regularly solicit proxies, see Reg. 14C. Subsequent proxy material: file preliminary copies at least 2 days before stockholder mailing. Definitive copies filed before mailing.	Immediate newspaper publicity on controversial issues, especially when there is a contest. Prompt notice to be received not later than 10 days before record date. Four copies definitive proxy material. Ask for advance review in major matters. (See Exchange rules.)
Redemption of Listed Securities	8-K.	8-K. Immediate press publicity. Prompt notice to Exchange not less than 15 days before redemption date.
Registration Statement	Involved legal proceedings and publicity practices. Consult legal counsel.	(See Col. 1.)
Revaluation of Assets or Restatement of Capital Share Account	8-K if material (company or significant subsidiaries).	8-K if filed. Prior supplement to listing agreement required for change in par value.
Rights to Subscribe	Registration under the Securities Act of 1933. Prefiling notice limited by SEC Rule 135.	See regulations. Preliminary discussion necessary —immediate publicity. Important to work out time schedule with Exchange before any action taken. Notice to shareholders not less than 10 days in advance of the proposed record date.

210

REPORTING REQUIREMENTS

American Stock Exchange	Midwest and Pacific Stock Exchange	Generally Recommended Publicity Practice— All Companies
Same as NYSE.	MIDWEST: Three copies definitive proxy material. PACIFIC: Four copies definitive proxy material.	TD: When a contest or non-routine matters involved. Normally publicity not needed on routine matters.
8-K. Same as NYSE.	8-K. Prompt publicity to holders and to Exchange a reasonable time in advance of redemption date.	TD: Usually advertisement is required. Written notice to security holders.
(See Col. 1.)	(See Col. 1.)	Publicity severely restricted. See applicable SEC releases.
8-K if filed. Prior notice of change of par value of stock split, file listing application.	8-K if filed. Same as NYSE.	Depending on circumstances.
Same as NYSE.	MIDWEST: Notify in time to afford holders an interim—satisfactory to Exchange—within which to record their interests to exercise their rights. Publish promptly to holders. PACIFIC: Immediate publicity. Ten days notice prior to record date.	TD

Reporting Required for	Securities and Exchange Commission	New York Stock Exchange
Stock Split or Other Change in Capitalization	8-K required for increase or decrease if exceeds five per cent of amount of securities of the class previously outstanding. IMPORTANT: Check with legal counsel.	For increase—copy of 8-K sufficient, except notice if through reissuance of previously reacquired listed securities. Issuance of additional amount requires prior listing approval. For decrease— see Redemption of Listed Securities and Treasury Stock Changes.
Treasury Stock— Increase or Decrease	Check Form 8-K, Items 7 and 8, for possible application.	8-K if filed. Notice within 10 days after close of fiscal quarter in which it takes place.

REPORTING REQUIREMENTS

American Stock Exchange	Midwest and Pacific Stock Exchange	Generally Recommended Publicity Practice— All Companies
Same as NYSE.	MIDWEST: Notify of any proposed increase sufficiently prior to permit action on application for listing. Also if issue securities on parity with or senior to listed securities. PACIFIC: Issuance of additional amount requires prior listing authorization.	TD: As soon as decision to put matter to vote of shareholders is made.
8-K if filed. Same as NYSE.	MIDWEST: 8-K if filed. Same as NYSE. PACIFIC: 8-K if filed. Notice within 15 days after close of fiscal quarter.	Normally no publicity.

You may ask for and expect to have these costs clearly outlined and explained in advance:

A fixed monthly retainer fee; a retainer plus monthly billing for actual staff time on an hourly or per diem basis; a base fee, billed monthly, to which are added increments for services performed beyond the retainer.

Out-of-pocket expenses are generally billed at cost and are exclusive of the fee.

When the public relations counseling firm is retained to handle individual or short term projects, it may quote a single fee for the work, plus an allowance for expenses.

Computers and Public Relations:
Fact vs Fancy
An Insider's View *

Public relations' use of the computer may seem a dichotomy. The public relations process is creative; the computer process is manipulative. The public relations process puts a premium on the ability to move quickly into new opportunities or to face new problems; the computer requires long lead times for systems work and programming. Public relations programs involve subtle change, very often imperceptible except over the longest period of time; computers deal only in hard, cold, measurable facts that are analyzable in a split second. The only answer to bridging this gap lies in the involvement of the public relations professional in computer technology.

And when the public relations man gets involved, he is likely to find enormous demands made of him.

First, he will learn that behind even the most casual request for computer-based data is oftentimes a mountain of statistics, research, demographics, and other facts that have to be gathered, sorted, classified, formatted, transcribed, stored, read, analyzed, re-stored, re-formatted, printed out, and delivered to the executive to help him make his decisions.

* Specially written for *An Executive's Primer on Public Relations* by Robert G. Strayton, director of public relations and merchandising, Honeywell, Inc., Electronic Data Processing division, Wellesley Hills, Mass.

214

So, it will very likely be decades before we are able to capture the types of data in which high confidence can be placed in making public relations decisions. There is the problem of valid demographic information. An entire research industry has been built up to develop this data. The most sophisticated users of it are several large advertising agencies. They make use of the demographics, combined with media research and frequency information, to generate media schedules. These schedules are most imposing to look at, but even the most bullish research director in the ad agency business will tell you to be wary of basing decisions on the computerized data before you. It contains a high degree of error, regardless of the purifying process it went through.

Demographics can be valuable tools for the public relations man, for they point to a general direction, but their characteristics are in the process of rapid evaluation and refinement.

Second, the element of psychographics is one that compounds the problem of demographic analysis. It has to do not with the statistical analysis of the consumer or typical message-recipient, but with his psychological characteristics. This discipline, now evolving rapidly, considers factors such as self-image, likes and dislikes, biases, timing factors and all the other intuitive and intellectual human processes that the public relations man, perhaps better than any other communicator, tries so hard to factor into his planning.

The computer can be of assistance in the development and analysis of psychographic and demographic data; its use in these areas can give public relations people far better views of the gross makeup of audience segments and sub-segments than have ever been seen before. And the computer can relate these data back to media lists, mailing lists, or other "people" groups that are of importance in an overall public relations program. Thus, the *relative* success of one program against another can be measured with good accuracy. The *actual* success of one program in attaining its specific objectives among specific audiences will continue for some time to be a measurement of human intuition and judgment rather than any computer process.

As we look ahead to the next decade, and it is indeed difficult to speculate beyond that, there are several areas where computers can be put to work effectively in public relations activities.

First, assuming that public relations is the umbrella term encompassing all forms of external communications, a computer can be used with excellent results to help balance the mix of various communication tools, to keep track of costs of using each tool, and to effectively handle budget-vs-expense items.

At Honeywell's EDP division we now use a computer for every one of these things, including helping us decide on the application of both financial and human resources to the areas of press relations, public affairs, community relations, exhibits, demonstrations, sales promotion, audio visual activities and advertising. The immediate availability of cost and time data in each of these areas makes it easier for department managers and project managers to make valid determinations of which resources to apply, where, at what time and at what expense, to achieve what end.

Second, we will see computers playing a major role in the speeded-up gathering of demographic data and program results. This will lead to almost immediate feedback on reactions to new campaigns, broken down by geographic and demographic characteristics. Such "instant replay" of a new communications program can be valuable, particularly to those executives who hold their breath every time a new communications program goes into effect. Instant replay with computer gathered data has already begun and will sweep the research business within the next 10 years as lower cost terminals, such as CRT's and Picturephones, are readily connectable at very low cost to a central computer system. The caveat that comes with "instant replay" is for making value judgments based on it. Sometimes time, not immediate replay, is the greatest ally of a good idea. But "instant replay" is here now in a small way and here to stay in a much bigger way in the future.

Third, the use of management science tools. One of the greatest areas in the computer industry, if not the greatest, is the current growth of interest by top management in applying the tools of what has come to be known as management science to their businesses. These tools are largely computer-based. They include linear programming, Pert, critical path method and simulation techniques. As the communications function within an organization comes to be recognized as a principal top management function, we will see these tools—which are now used every day to help solve problems like locating plants, setting up distribution systems, developing new-product cycles and performing financial analyses—used in the communications area as well. It is for that reason that public relations management is going to have to take the painful step, already taken by many top executives, of getting involved in computer technology.

Fourth, the computer today is and will continue to be a production tool in the communications mix. It is capable now of maintaining and printing out endless types of mailing lists. It can actually generate computer-produced letters that are personalized to the point of using the addressee's name in several places in the letter's text. It can be used for rough measurements of "exposure" by correlating the content of the message, its distribution, and the available characteristics of the probable audience that was exposed to it. It handles expense statements and media analysis with dispatch.

It is not a question of whether computers will be used in the PR business. It is only a question of how much usage, how fast, in what ways and by whom. A public relations man will never know, unless he gets involved now in finding out about this important new tool.

SOME PLAIN TALK ON MAKING SPEECHES

As chief executive, whether you revel in or rebel against making speeches, it's part of the ceremonial routine of the job. The deep, silent type of corporate executive pretty much went out of style when stockholders first began to ask what was happening to their money, more than 100 years ago.

If you've made the proper choice of public relations executive, he can be of immeasurable help in this chore; but make no mistake, he cannot transform you into a Demosthenes or imbue you with the platform presence and wit of Adlai Stevenson. You've got to do some homework. The best basic training you can absorb is to understand what is involved in making an effective speech, and the steps you must take to reach that level of performance.

Possibly you're an old hand at this; then this review may simply serve to remind you of building stages that you probably now perform intuitively. But, perhaps you've made speeches only "now and then," with indifferent success, in which case this review will have more pertinence.

But whether you're a pro or a rank amateur, a few minutes spent reviewing such basics as how to hold your audience, how to put across a punch line, and how to end with a bang, will be time well-invested. Maybe you've fallen into some careless habits born of repeated exposure, or maybe you just need these pointers to take off the rough edges and give you the poise and confidence you're really capable of.

HOW TO GET READY

First, let's make one thing clear. Public speaking can be learned only by public speaking. And whatever pearls of rhetoric your public relations man weaves for you, it is you,

218

not he, who must present them. It's been said a million times, and probably needs saying another million, but public speaking cannot be done by reading a book on the subject, and that includes these pages.

It's important to realize this, so that you don't become too critical of yourself, especially if it's your first real talk. The second will be better, more polished, easier to do; the third will be better than the second, and so on. Like swimming, driving a car, or playing golf, you'll learn by doing.

Obviously, before you venture forth, you or your public relations man will have to do some spadework. He'll need to get the facts in order, to work out a flow of thoughts or points to insure even continuity, so that you don't ramble all over the lot and bury your principal points in a sea of disjointed semantics.

You're probably envious of the man who can stand up, without a note, and spiel off a beautiful, witty, flowing, interesting talk, whether it's for five minutes or twenty-five. You can rest assured that he has put in many, many long hours of preparation to be able to achieve that effortless grace. The Dale Carnegie folks, who have probably coached more people in the art of public speaking than any other group, say flatly that there is no such thing as an extemporaneous, or ad lib speech. It may seem that way, but you can be sure that the speaker has carefully worked it all out beforehand. It's experience and practice, and anticipation that enable him to stand up and talk without a single note in sight.

Self-confidence is a by-product of thorough preparation.

NO GETTING OUT OF AN OUTLINE

Every executive has his own work style—and in something as personal to him as his own speech, it's best to stick to the formula most comfortable to him. Some executives like to draft the first version themselves, then turn it over to their public relations man for editing, criticizing or polishing; others prefer to talk it over with their public relations man and come to some agreement on approach, content and thrust. Still others prefer to wait until they see what the public relations man has developed, then build or re-build on this.

Of the three, the middle course leads to the best results —the first tends to wed the executive to his own words and thoughts so rigidly that there's no room for constructive criticism; the last course often wastes time, shortens tempers and creates more work rather than easing it. Even if the public relations executive *is* virtually an alter ego of the chief executive, he cannot always fully know the depth of feeling the chief executive may have on a subject nor know fully his train of thought, which often changes with the conditions of the speech, the audience, the environment, etc.

If the chief executive, once committed to making a speech, gives some thought to it *before* having a session with his adviser, it will ultimately turn out to be a better talk. This can be an almost subliminal effort, perhaps just ruminating over it while commuting, or shaving. Then, turn off the phones for a half-hour or so and go over the ideas with your public relations adviser. Agree upon a basic approach. Depending on your relationship with him (some public relations men can pick up the precise tone an executive wants to give a talk from five minutes of chatting; others proceed less spontaneously but nonetheless successfully with a more methodical approach), you may or may not want a written outline. Generally, it's not a bad idea in any case; it helps enormously in plotting the beginning, the middle and the closing. Elementary? Of course, but it's a detail to which a polished speaker should never be too over-confident to pay homage.

A good speech is built like a house, sentence by sentence; don't, therefore, expect the first draft turned in by your public relations expert to be the quintessence of the art. It'll probably take many drafts; have patience, and go over each with him; don't shoot it back via interoffice with some nearly undecipherable scratchings on it.

SAY SOMETHING

Don't be naïve about your speech. Don't let the title they've given you inhibit you. It is not really intended to limit you to that subject and that alone. As a matter of fact, one of the more boring speeches in political oratory came when a prominent eastern governor, invited to address a fund-raising banquet on behalf of muscular dystrophy, did just that: spoke on muscular dystrophy, to the dismay of a packed audience of $100-a-plate diners.

You can cover the subject and still have room to make a few points of your own; one should flow logically from the other, of course.

But as corporate officer, representing the company more than yourself, you can best amortize the time and money invested in the occasion by using it to attract favorable regard for the company, to the degree that you can reflect this. So, say something thought-provoking; make 'em listen, think (maybe even wake up). Stir them up a bit, even at the risk of generating some disagreement.

This doesn't mean an open license to be provocative, hang the cost. There's a limitless inventory of subjects worthy of public discussion. For example, we're currently having a revival of the middle ages' town-and-gown upheavals and students vs administration dispute. Doesn't this suggest a talk in which the roles of dissent, protest and civil disobedience might each be put into proper perspective? Let's skip Vietnam; that's too political. But certainly the question of how much and how far to go in urban rehabilitation,

221

wiping out pockets of poverty, opens room for stimulating discussion. Perhaps you have a company deep in technology and the space-age; forecasts of the twenty-first century will surely not be dull; but you might take a different tack and predict, one way or another, whether or not there will be any measurable civilian fall-off from space-age technology.

A not untypical example of what can be made of a seemingly cut-and-dried speaking engagement is illustrated by an experience of T. Mitchell Ford, president of Emhart Corporation. He was asked to officiate and say "a few words" at a small graduation ceremony at a Connecticut vocational school. Rather than brush-off the obligation superficially, Ford asked his staff for suggestions for items of pertinent comment. Research disclosed the fact that vocational schools were laboring under a form of second-class educational citizenship, despite the fact that millions of young people unable to go to college would lean on their resources. This set the theme of the brief remarks: that for the 7 million teen-age high school drop-outs, plus the two million who will never even get that far in this decade, vocational, or occupational training offers the only practical avenue for the economic freedom that education can provide. Comment on the talk received wide news coverage, with excerpts carried in such important media as the *Wall Street Journal*.

The measure of the success of the occasion lies not in interpreting this as a publicity ploy, but rather in a demonstration of leadership in bringing to light a serious social problem. It more than amortizes the time and effort taken from a corporate day to perform what otherwise seems only a routine ceremonial function of the office of president.

If it's worth *your* time to make an appearance, it's worth your public relations adviser's time to make certain that you say something that will be of as much interest in Chicago as it is in Newark, or as much in San Francisco as it was in New York.

222

NOTES OR TEXT—
THE LONG AND SHORT OF IT

Speeches rarely "talk" as well as they "read," so the debate waxes whether or not it is best to write out the full text, or simply to use brief outline notes as reminders of points to be covered. Again, this is a matter of personal style and comfort.

Some executives can read a speech easily; they look up frequently, break down sentences into bites that most clearly follow normal conversation patterns, and generally do a creditable job. Often, for policy reasons, too, an executive must follow a specific text. The experts suggest that if you are planning to read your speech that you do it aloud, privately, several times; some even say do this in front of a mirror, so that you can practice looking up at the audience.

If you have a fairly good memory and enough self-confidence, then after you've run through the complete text several times, translate the main points to an outline or topical listing. Practice re-constructing the speech with only these brief notes as a guide.

Then, when you bring them back to memory in your talk, they will be more obviously *your words* and *your thoughts,* since you will unconsciously put them into your own phraseology as you would talk, not as you would write.

Following are some fundamental pointers, whether you use the long form or the short:

Don't be afraid to digress. This breaks up the pat evenness of a speech, gives it a spontaneity that sparks interest. Maybe it's a story that comes to mind as you've made a point, or a quote you'd like to read, to expand or substantiate another point. Whatever it is, do it.

No jargon, please. Businessmen have a gobbledygook and jargon of their own; it's a sort of overstuffed prose that favors bloated, pseudo-formal phraseology like "terminate" instead of "end," "in the aggregate" rather than "total," etc. Speak naturally; that business correspondence style makes for cold, formal speeches.

Look like a pro. I'm sure you wouldn't wear a sport coat, but for the record, don't. A dark, conservative suit, of course. After you've been introduced and have acknowledged the introduction, stand squarely behind the podium (if there is one; if not, in the center of the stage, platform, or what have you). Stand erect (not at attention; but don't lounge); don't fidget, lean over or on the podium (this marks an amateur) or move around. If there's a mike, remember you don't have to aim your voice at it; it's sensitive enough to pick up your voice if you talk naturally 12 to 15 inches away. Just make sure your voice is directed at it and not to the side of the microphone.

Talk to everybody. There's an old speech-maker's rule that says single out one person in the audience and talk to him. Do that and you're liable to make both him and you uneasy. Better to skip around the audience; direct your attention to different parts of the room. At least you'll look like you're talking to everybody.

Smile. Making the speech may be a burden to you, but think of the audience; they have to listen. Least you can do is smile; don't look glum and tip 'em off that the worst is yet to come. Smiles are infectious; use some.

Shift gears once in a while. Nothing's so boring as a speaker with only one speed—one tone of voice. Change your inflections, raise and lower your voice to make a point or to emphasize something.

You may never have seen Billy Sunday speak, but you've no doubt watched Billy Graham, his modern-day counterpart in speech-making. Men of this type are past masters in the art of making a speech, and the art of gestures. (Among the politicians, Hubert Humphrey and Senator

224

Everett Dirksen personify stylish public speakers, versed in using the whole anatomy and voice to animate a speech.)

This isn't a license to jump around, gesticulating like a witch doctor, but don't stand there like a wooden statue with a built-in tape recorder.

A little humor. Jokes are fine, if they're reasonably fresh—and appropriate to the occasion. Don't strain; no one expects you to be as quick on the quip as Bob Hope or George Burns. And don't, for heaven's sake, use any of the garden-variety jokes, jokes clipped from one of the jokes-for-every-occasion books. Remember the best ones your friends have told you; get in the habit of clipping the best ones you read in a paper or magazine; categorize them (i.e., openers, closers, dedications, etc.) and put them in an envelope against the time you'll need one or two.

The best jokes are those that you can make a personal experience. You may stretch the truth a little here, but it's a liberty all speakers take.

Finally, don't open by saying, "I've a joke to tell you, etc." If it's funny, they'll know it was a joke without your telling them.

YOU'RE THE KING

Now, you're all set to go.

As you stand up and look out over the sea of faces, remember that you're the King. They came here to listen to you! You know more about your subject than they do, so what are you worrying about, anyway?

Who cares if you're not a polished speaker? Just be yourself. Be sincere, know what you're talking about (that's what the practice and the outline were all about), smile—and you're home free!

FOR FURTHER STUDY ON BACKGROUND AND PERSPECTIVE

Bernays, Edward L., *Crystallizing Public Opinion,* Liveright Publishing Corp., New York, 1961.

Brayman, Harold, *Corporate Management in a World of Politics,* McGraw-Hill Book Company, New York, 1967.

Burton, Paul, *Corporate Public Relations,* Reinhold Publishing Corp., New York, 1966.

Golden, L. L. L., *Only by Public Consent,* Hawthorn Books, Inc., New York, 1968.

Marston, John, *The Nature of Public Relations,* McGraw-Hill Book Company, New York, 1963.

Miller, Robert W., *Corporate Policies and Public Attitudes,* The American University Press, Washington, D.C., 1965.

Riley, John W., Jr., *The Corporation and Its Publics: Essays on the Corporate Image,* John Wiley & Sons, Inc., New York, 1963.

Simon, Raymond, *Perspectives in Public Relations,* University of Oklahoma Press, Norman, Oklahoma, 1966.

Whyte, William H. and the Editors of *Fortune, Is Anybody Listening,* Simon and Schuster, Inc., New York, 1952.

Wright, Theon and Henry S. Evans, *Public Relations and the Line Manager,* American Management Association, Inc., New York, 1964.

MORE ON THE SPECIFICS

Beveridge, Oscar M., *Financial Public Relations,* McGraw-Hill Book Company, New York, 1963.

Darrow, Richard W., Dan J. Forrestal, and Aubrey O. Cookman, *Public Relations Handbook,* The Dartnell Corporation, Chicago, Ill., 1967.

Davison, W. Phillips, *International Political Communication,* Frederick A. Praeger, Inc., New York, 1965.

Foster, LeBaron R., *Telling the Company's Financial Story,* Financial Executives Research Foundation, New York, 1964.

Hill & Knowlton, International, *Handbook on International Public Relations,* Vol. I, Frederick A. Praeger, Inc., New York, 1968.

Robinson, Dr. Edward L., *Communications and Public Relations,* Charles E. Merrill Publishing Co., Columbus, Ohio, 1966.

Thomas, Ella Cooper, *The Law of Libel and Slander,* Oceana Publications, Inc., Dobbs Ferry, New York, 1963.

ON COUNSELING

Prentice-Hall, *Inside Public Relations,* Prentice-Hall, Inc., Englewood Cliffs, New Jersey, 1963.

ADDITIONAL SOURCE MATERIAL

A Public Relations Bibliography (Second Edition), Scott M. Cutlip, University of Wisconsin Press, Madison, Wisconsin, 1965.

The Public Relations Journal (monthly), 845 Third Avenue, New York.

The PR Reporter (weekly), PR Publishing Company, Meriden, New Hampshire.

Public Relations News (weekly), 129 E. 80th Street, New York.

The Public Relations Quarterly, 305 E. 45th Street, New York.

Who's Who in Public Relations, PR Publishing Company, Meriden, New Hampshire.

Index

231

About the Author

John F. Budd, Jr., Group Vice President, and member of The Executive Staff, Carl Byoir & Associates, was Publicity Director for the New York Museum of Science & Industry prior to joining Byoir. Before that, he was Sales Promotion-Publicity Representative for Northeast Airlines, New York. In twenty years of service at Byoir, he has handled, conceived and directed national and international public relations programs for seven major corporations. These assignments range from financial and investor relations to new product promotion, to community and civil rights activity. They include development of the program for the international introduction of an electronic wrist timepiece; a nationwide preview, via closed-circuit TV, of a $35-million aerospace research center; creation of a comprehensive supplier support program, and a national program supporting a new corporate entity's entry into the electronic computer field. He has developed and supervised new plant opening programs for four companies in as many states, including the unveiling of a $50-million papermaking complex on the West Coast.

Programs that he conceived and directed were judged "outstanding" by the Public Relations Society of America in 1964 and 1965, and were given top national recognition; another was cited by *PR News* for annual achievement, in 1957. He has lectured on public relations at Adelphi University and Hofstra University, where he is a trustee and member of The Board's Executive Committee, and has written a number of articles and addressed a number of groups on the subject. More than a half million copies of his two booklets on automation and space technology terms have been distributed.